THE WINNING FORMULA

DAVID COULTHARD

THE WINNING FORMULA

BLINK

bringing you closer

Published by Blink Publishing
2.25, The Plaza,
535 Kings Road,
Chelsea Harbour,
London, SW10 0SZ

www.blinkpublishing.co.uk

facebook.com/blinkpublishing
twitter.com/blinkpublishing

Hardback – 978-1788700-11-5
Trade Paperback – 978-1788700-12-2
Ebook – 978-1788700-10-8

A CIP catalogue of this book is available from the British Library.

Designed by seagulls.net
Printed and bound by Clays Ltd, Elcograf S.p.A.

3 5 7 9 10 8 6 4 2

Blink Publishing is an imprint of the Bonnier Publishing Group
www.bonnierpublishing.co.uk

For Karen

CONTENTS

INTRODUCTION

I was sitting in front of Dietrich Mateschitz in his offices in Salzburg, about to sign for his new F1 team, a decision that represented one of the biggest risks of my career. The billionaire founder of Red Bull is an imposing man, a remarkable entrepreneur with a hugely successful energy drinks company, and a laser-like focus. He had never previously been the sole owner of an F1 team but had recently bought Jaguar F1 for $1. Intrigued by that development, I had been in discussions for some time about joining this new team. Having driven for established teams such as Williams and McLaren, joining Dietrich's new organisation was a gamble, and one that would secure me a significant pay cut, too. But it felt right, it felt exciting and my gut instinct was telling me that this was an opportunity not to be missed…

. . .

When I walked off the racing circuit at Brazil in 2004, for all intents and purposes, my racing career in Formula 1 was over. I had been with McLaren for nine years but that famous team had recently decided not to renew my contract, so it appeared that the curtain might be coming down on my time in the sport I loved. Back at the start of the year, along with my contracts manager, Martin Brundle, I'd been talking to Jaguar Racing, but through all the discussions I just didn't sense the passion or vision that I need to really commit to a new venture. Ultimately, I didn't have the belief that joining Jaguar would work for me. I even did a list with Martin in my apartment of the pros and cons of joining that team and there were a lot more cons than pros.

I still felt I had a lot to offer so after deciding against Jaguar, I spoke to a number of other more established teams. Renault, Ferrari and Williams had already filled their race seats, so I asked about testing for them, but to no avail. Fast-forward to the end of the year and after Red Bull bought Jaguar, Christian Horner and Helmut Marko quickly came on board as part of an impressive team-management structure and so, almost overnight, what had previously been an uninspiring option suddenly became an opportunity that was potentially hugely interesting to me. Initial talks went well, and I was subsequently invited to take part in a test at Jerez, which is when I first met Dietrich Mateschitz.

Speaking to Dietrich at trackside in Jerez, I was immediately struck by how focused, energised and determined he was to make his first foray into overall team ownership a total success. We talked about the resources needed to do that and he didn't baulk when I mentioned possible numbers. He clearly had experience in F1 already, having been a part of the Sauber management team for some time, but this was the first time he would be sole owner. I came away from that meeting hugely impressed and noticeably excited by the vision he and his team had proposed. Nonetheless, this was a far from straightforward choice. Dietrich certainly knew my industry but, in theory, for me to jump across to racing for a team with no front grid experience and only a very limited history in the sport was a big risk. In addition to the significant pay cut, there was absolutely no guarantee that I wouldn't just end up in an inferior car, racing from the back of the grid, week after week.

However, I just didn't see it like that. Here was a man with ideas and acumen; Dietrich's own staggering success with Red Bull speaks for itself. In terms of his approach to F1, he had empowered his team to start revitalising the struggling operation he had bought; in turn, they were keen to attract both established talent as well as nurture new motorsport brains; they were also open to investing the sort of resources Formula 1 requires and accumulatively this created a very attractive package that I was strongly drawn to. There just seemed like so many strong and promising business and motorsports elements coming together that it was hard not to be impressed.

So with the contracts agreed, I travelled to Dietrich's Salzburg offices to sign the documents. I'd taken him a gift of a Theo Fennel replica of a Red Bull can that I'd had made in silver with no lid, as a pencil holder for his desk. That was an idea actually inspired by Bernie Ecclestone, who had the very classy ritual of sending every race driver a silver telegram when they'd won their first grand prix, a stylish gesture that I duplicated here, hopefully to remind Dietrich of our meeting in the years to come.

As you can probably imagine, Mateschitz is a very impressive individual and sitting in his office that day I could sense that this was not a project that was going to fail. During our conversation, I pointed out that as part of my lower salary race package I had been given badges on my suit and helmet that I was allowed to sell to sponsors to increase my income. Now, I had no intention of selling those spaces so in that Salzburg meeting I said to Dietrich, 'Regarding these badges, I'm assuming you don't want me selling them to Bananas R Us or put some lurid airline logos on there?' He said he didn't want that and immediately offered to buy back the spaces. Simple, mutually beneficial, efficient.

My gut instinct was telling me that joining Red Bull was the right thing to do. Did I know at that point that I was joining a team that would go on to win four World Drivers' and Constructors' Championships? No, but like a lot of things in sport, business and life, you do your research, you weigh up the risks and the rewards, and then you back your instincts and make your decision. Multiple world titles would suggest that I made the right call. So I signed the contracts and began racing for Red Bull.

• • •

The success story of Mateschitz and Red Bull is a classic example of so many of the topics that I want to discuss in this book. Being a part of Red Bull's fantastic achievements was exhilarating and exciting, but it also taught me so much, just as the sport of Formula 1 has over the years. I have been fortunate to work for many years in an environment surrounded by highly driven individuals – Sir Frank Williams, Ron Dennis, Ayrton Senna, Alain Prost, Adrian Newey, Christian Horner, Dietrich Mateschitz, Sir Patrick Head, Michael Schumacher, Nigel Mansell and many more – how can I have failed to learn from them?

Away from Formula 1, the learning never ends. I've been fortunate enough to enjoy a post-racing career in the media, as well as hotels and several other areas of business. One of those new career avenues that I thoroughly enjoy is speaking at conferences and events, along with my friend, motorsport businessman Mark Gallagher. On our travels around the globe I have been constantly amazed at the mistakes, inefficient attitudes and basic business failings of apparently experienced and intelligent people. These ideas and themes seem to be constantly reappearing, like an international code for how to – or how not to – approach business. That was in part the driving force behind deciding to write this book.

Sport is inspirational, it brings people together but ultimately it is also a business. So it follows that you can learn from the business of sport and apply those lessons in your own career, company or business. Through sporting examples and analogies along with my own experiences, I hope you will be able to see why universal themes such as a hard work ethic, unleashing your personal potential, the power of the team, customer service, innovation and efficiency, attention to detail and the relentless pursuit of marginal gains are all essential and healthy ideas… and not just for a racing driver from the south-west corner of Scotland.

CHAPTER 1
WORK ETHIC

Formula 1 is famous for long, anti-social hours and a very demanding working life. It is a sport populated by people from all corners of the globe who are extremely driven and, above all else, immensely hard-working. That is why you hear the drivers in their post-race interviews thanking all the people 'back at the factory', because they know exactly how much effort by so many behind-the-scenes team members has gone in to securing a podium or win. In Formula 1, it is a given that you are prepared to work *very* hard.

You often overhear people saying how hard they've been working but, of course, the definition of 'hard work' can differ enormously from the one person to another. Some people are more driven than others. I believe I have a strong work ethic and that without this I would not have achieved a fraction of what I did in F1 or indeed since.

It was easy for me to learn about the importance of having a strong work ethic because my parents were the perfect examples.

Back when I was a wee lad, my parents taught me the most simple and essential lesson: without a hard work ethic, you have no foundations for anything in sport, business and, indeed, life.

I was born into the third generation of an entrepreneurial Scottish family and grew up in the small village of Twynholm, in Dumfries and Galloway in the south-west corner of Scotland, home to a few hundred people. Although the area is very rural, my great-grandfather started a haulage company there over 100 years ago, which my grandfather and father developed, and my brother runs to this day, all hard-working people. Hayton Coulthard remains one of the most well-known of all haulage firms in the UK, and celebrated its centenary in 2016.

By the time my father was a young lad, the family business was well established and provided a secure income, although the Coulthards were still very much a working-class family. My grandfather was always very busy; he was a racer too, running at the Tulip Rally in an old Austin Sheerline and he even competed in the Monte Carlo Rally. Consequently, my father was surrounded by motor-racing and lucky enough to see the greats, such as Jim Clark, Jackie Stewart and Graham Hill, in the heat of battle. Perhaps inevitably, he started racing and found he was exceptionally talented, eventually becoming the Scottish karting champion. So I was born into a family that was used to hard work, looking after the haulage business, and having these amateur racing careers, too.

Tragically, my grandfather died aged just 44, when my dad was only 14. Aside from the grief and emotional trauma, the loss effectively ended my dad's racing career as he now had to focus on the family business. As a child, he was dyslexic and also something of a loner at school, so his days were never easy. Back then dyslexia wasn't understood in the way it is today, and he tells the story of how at the end of every term they would all 'line up behind Coulthard' to get the belt, because it was always assumed that he would be getting punished first. However, although he struggled with the more academic work, Father threw himself into sports – so much so that he eventually won the 'Victor Ludorum' award. I'm not going to pretend I know Latin, but I believe that translates as 'The Winner of The Games'. He was never going to be a science geek so his way of finding success was through sport and he worked very hard at that. You need to find your path to success.

Back at home the real work started. He would help out with the business, working late whenever it was needed. At the age of 17 he also took a job driving the local parcel lorry to bring in extra money. He became an apprentice mechanic, drove the lorries, and would eventually learn all the jobs in the office, too. His father had stipulated that at the age of 21 my father would take over, but when he came of age and was given the keys to the business, the company was not financially successful. It's very easy to mess up a business when you are handed control at such a young age, but Father met the challenge head-on, and tackled it as he always does – with hard work and dedication.

He tells a great story about how, when he first took over the company, every day was a challenge. One night he was at home, trying to think of ways of generating new business and he went to the kitchen to get something to eat. He opened a cupboard and there was a solitary can of Heinz Beans inside. Instead of looking at that single tin and feeling sorry for himself, he instead looked at the telephone number on the side, phoned Heinz up and said, 'Can I speak to, oh… your transport manager, please forgive me, I forget his name… Mr…' to which the receptionist said, 'Mr Smith?' My father replied, 'Yes, of course, that's it, Mr Smith. Can I speak with Mr Smith please?' Obviously, my father had no idea who Mr Smith was.

She put him through and when Mr Smith came on the phone my father said, 'I've heard you've had some difficulties with your distribution from Scotland…' In fact, my father hadn't heard any such thing but it created a conversation that led to a meeting, and that, in turn, kicked off a long-standing and very productive relationship between Heinz and my father's company.

When my father got together with my mother, she gave him additional strength and the two of them cracked on and created a hugely successful business. They were married in their very early twenties, and with Dad in charge of the family business, they simply rolled up their sleeves and got on with it.

My mother's dad was a train driver and her mum a nurse, very much a working-class family who had to put in the hours every day just to put food on the table. My mother is one of eight kids so hers was a household that was constantly busy, to say the least. As a team, my parents were formidable and I learnt so much from them about business and life. My father was always bouncing ideas off my mother and that's how they built the business up; in fact, I mirror my parents' relationship with my wife, Karen, as I will often present various options to her and we talk ideas through in detail.

They were flat out all the time. I am one of three children and when my older brother Duncan was very young, they would go out in their little MG sports car complete with nappies and a bucket, scouring for new business. Sometimes they'd drive as far afield as London, stay with the baby in a £2-a-night room (the cheapest, because it was the nightwatchman's), do the meetings and then head all the way home to Twynholm. With a baby in tow, that's quite a feat!

My parents were determined that their children understood the value of money and, crucially, how much hard work was needed to create success and wealth. As much as I didn't particularly enjoy it at the time, during my pre-teenage years I did the odd holiday job, such as working on local farms collecting potatoes (or 'tattie picking', as we would call it in Scotland) and cleaning people's cars.

I started racing at a young age, after my father bought me a basic 100cc kart for my 11th birthday. This is relatively late for a future Formula 1 driver – for example, Mika Häkkinen started aged just five and Lewis Hamilton started around the age of seven. Even so, despite being a relative late-comer, I seemed to have an element of talent. Practically, and for the purposes of this chapter, my blossoming karting career was a big commitment for my parents on top of everything else they had to contend with, but to meet that challenge their work rate just went up another notch. At first the racing was mostly local, within a two-hour drive of home, all relatively nearby or perhaps just a modest journey. However, as I progressed quickly and started winning, the competitions we needed to enter were all over Britain (I won the Scottish Karting Championship three times, by which time the sport had completely taken over my life). If you think of where Twynholm is in south-west Scotland, that demands a lot of driving. London, for example, was over 370 miles away. We had a motorhome which we pretty much lived in, and the mileage we did was incredible. Remember, my parents had a thriving and extremely busy haulage business to attend to, as well as ferrying me around.

Of course, you can't just turn up to a race at the weekend and expect to win. Week nights required plenty of preparation. Monday nights were for unpacking and cleaning the motorhome; Tuesday would see us strip the kart and check it all over; Wednesday would be used for maintenance of the leathers, helmet and other safety gear; Thursday would be the night for packing the motorhome ahead of the weekend; Fridays would often be a pick-up straight from school if the race was a long way down south, without a chance to change out of my blazer and uniform.

Even if the race was more local, a typical weekend would see us get up very early Saturday morning to drive to the track for practice sessions. We'd work on the kart all day, making sure everything was in order and working correctly, then the races would be on the Sunday so at some point we'd head off for the long journey to the circuit. For my parents, the effort and commitment required was relentless. They would be off on the road seeing clients for the transport company for much of the week, working very long hours, and then we'd have these manic weekends, driving to a race somewhere hundreds of miles away, karting all weekend, and only get home in the wee small hours of Monday morning. It was also a lot of work for a teenage lad, although I think the effort I had to make just to get to the start line made me more focused – lads who lived an hour or so away from a circuit could just turn up and race. Easy, yes, but I think that maybe gave them a false sense of how much work was needed to get to the very top. On some occasions, of course, the race didn't go well and I might crash off early. When that happened, the drive home back to Twynholm felt like a very long way but it is just what we all did, that was the effort that was required. Even if we arrived home really late, we'd all have to haul the gear back to the house (my parents' home is on the top of a hill, accessible only by a footpath). 'No one comes up to the house empty-handed,' as my father decreed. Then a few brief hours of sleep later, I'd go to school and they would go straight to work. Unbelievable. With every year of progress in karting, the work required grew in size. As my national success escalated, I then moved up to racing in Europe, so the mileage and hard work ramped up many more levels. My parents' commitment to creating an opportunity for me was frankly astonishing, so having seen the lengths they went to for my benefit, I simply could not be lazy. Any success they have had in their life is in part because they've rolled their sleeves up and got on with the task in hand.

This strong work ethic extended to every area of our lives. My mother has always been very house proud and at home we all had to muck in and help, no matter how busy or tired we were. That was her way of showing us what to do, 'Keep your house clean, neat and tidy.' Consequently, I am pretty fastidious to this day, I like things to be neat, clean and well maintained.

In the week, my parents would be running the business, then they would drive down south for hundreds of miles to meet customers, then work on the karting at the weekends. The transport industry is not a nine-to-five business, it is 24 hours a day, there are trucks running all the time. Maybe a truck would break down or something would go wrong, and if that was late at night my parents couldn't afford to be on answerphone. When they left the office, the phones were diverted to the home landline, so that if there was a problem it would be dealt with whatever the time of day or night; it was normal in my house to have the phone ring at any hour. I was used to seeing my father doing work at the dinner table; he would come in from work and pretty much straight away sit for hours working out routes for the trucks, even though he had been up and in the office at the crack of dawn. As well as helping my father at work, my mother would also always make all the meals for everyone in the motorhome at the karting, cook and then freeze the food in advance, as well as collecting the kids from school and running the household, too. My mother was also heavily involved in the customer interaction, and that could be very long hours for her, because she'd get us all to school first thing, then work in the day, then sort us out after school, then there'd be customer dinner parties and events until late at night. These were long, gruelling days for both of them.

When it came to racing I naturally applied the work ethic I'd seen in my parents. I was very particular about keeping my kart absolutely immaculate. When I was cleaning the kart or the motorhome during the week and getting ready to go racing, my father would come and inspect what I had done. I had no problem with that, it certainly wasn't a feeling of, 'Oh crap, here he comes,' because I knew I'd done a good job. Besides, there was a logic and motivation to my working so hard at keeping my kart clean. I was not cleaning a certain small part for it to look pretty, I was doing it so that I could look at that part up close. If you clean something, you look at it; if you look at it, you might see any signs of wear and fatigue or actual damage. I used to polish the underside of my racing cars, put them up on a ramp and polish the aluminium floor with Autosol paste. Nobody saw that floor except me but I knew that car in its entirety, every single rivet, and was constantly examining it in detail, so that if anything had come loose it would be spotted. That's what was needed, so I just got on with it.

This family trait also stood me in great stead once I graduated into more senior motorsport. This is a world where maximum effort is a given. F1 is the epitome of this. Everyone understands the pressures and if a task needs doing, people don't clock off at 5pm and leave. They stay until it is done. And, rather like many modern businesses, Formula 1 has some added problems, such as the fact that we have our headquarters in Europe but are racing all over the world, so we need everyone in the team to work across time zones, especially when the heat is on. If we have a problem at the track in Suzuka, Japan, we want to be able to get information or perhaps even upgraded components from the factory, despite there being an eight-hour time difference and a 12-hour flight for anyone who has to bring the parts out. So we don't expect everyone to have gone home at 5.30 in that case. The culture is therefore to work as a team, across time zones if necessary, even if this means that on some occasions it will require a very early start or a late night to give the team a chance of doing the best job. That's the culture of Formula 1.

With respect to my racing career, I can see very clearly how the work ethic instilled in me as a child benefited me as an adult racing driver. Okay, I was not the best racing driver of all time but I was able to sustain a career at the top for 15 years, win Grands Prix and drive nine of those years with McLaren, not because I was the best but because I had a relentless work ethic.

If we are all of equal talent and equal skill, and in theory competing on an equal playing field, then the element that is going to make one of us win through in the end is work ethic. The desire to get up and tackle that next mile like it's the first time you've done it, with the same energy and the same enthusiasm, without becoming jaded... that's how true champions are able to win year after year. Elite, record-breaking success is not necessarily God-given, lucky or accidental, but is framed by a relentless drive to improve and succeed. An individual needs prodigious talent but that needs to be backed up by application and work. Champions are able to apply an acute focus to get to the top and then stay there because they retain their hunger, they never dilute their work ethic, they maintain all the elements that got them to the chequered flag in the first place. You will not find a high-level athlete in any sport who hasn't worked relentlessly for years. Those who stop working hard when they get to the top don't stay there very long.

Michael Schumacher is a great example; with seven World Championships to his name, he has won more world titles than any other Formula 1 driver. Maybe in time that will change but for now he is top of the tree. It is also a fact that anyone in the paddock will verify that his work ethic was *legendary*.

When people were thinking he would be on the beach, Michael would in fact be on the test track. Late at night while other drivers were out at restaurants or socialising, you would find Michael at the factory; when others were still asleep very early in the morning or not yet in at work, he would already be at the headquarters, spending time with the team, showing people that he cared, and therefore that he wanted them to care. There were stories that he would turn up at the Ferrari head-quarters in Maranello on a non-Grand Prix weekend just to see who was in the office and chat to them, motivating them to work harder and achieve a higher degree of performance. His own application – to testing, fitness, development, leading by example – was painstaking.

Of course, this can come at a cost. Ultimately people who are this focused and driven may spend less time with their families, but Michael was prepared to go the extra mile to be the best. The record books show what he achieved. If you want to see an example of the extreme work ethic required to be a world class Formula 1 driver, look no further than Michael.

A current example that the more cynical of you might be surprised to hear about in terms of work ethic is multiple world champion Lewis Hamilton. In 2017, I travelled back from the Mexico GP with his Mercedes teammate Valtteri Bottas, just after Lewis had won his fourth driver's title and I asked, 'How is it working with Lewis?' and Valtteri replied, 'Man, I didn't realise he worked so hard.' With Lewis, there is an external perception that he is always at parties and fashion shows, that he is not focused, and this kind of criticism is in the papers all the time. Yet Valtteri said that when Lewis is at the track and in the factory, his focus and attention to detail and the job in hand is *second to none*. This should come as no surprise, since we know results come from the application put in. You don't achieve what Lewis has without putting in the hard yards. What people need to understand about Lewis is that when he is at the race track or the factory, he is totally switched on, and I mean *totally*. There are no parties or distractions. I have never met an engineer during the whole time Lewis has been racing, from a young kid up to the current day, who has worked with him and said, 'Lewis has got the talent but he doesn't work hard enough.' Away from the track, you don't get a physique like that without putting in an awful lot of hours in the gym. He has a great ability to compartmentalise the work he needs to do with the team and the car, and separate that from his private life. Part of being a successful racing driver is actually not being 'on' all the time, there has to be rest and recuperation, and Lewis seems able to strike that balance very, very well. His time-management is superb, his effort to keep supremely fit is obvious, his focus at the track is exemplary.

For my own part, I think the reasons I stayed at McLaren for nine seasons was not because I was faster than Mika Häkkinen or necessarily more naturally talented, but because I worked incredibly hard – relentlessly, consistently, always. I turned up at the tests without fail, I was in the car as often as I was able, I gave detailed and enthusiastic feedback, I showed up for sponsor events and made a real effort; I *cared*. Not every race driver takes that approach. Someone like Juan Pablo Montoya, for example, was a talented racing driver. He is also a person who some would say was a little irreverent and, to be fair, to many people that is part of his charm. However, he had a relatively short F1 career, likewise in Indy and NASCAR. Now he may be entirely fulfilled with those shorter careers but for someone who is considered a very naturally talented driver, why does nothing quite stick?

The best part about having a hard work ethic is that it isn't rocket science. Just get up bright and early every day and get on; ask the question, 'Is there anything more I can be doing today?' If there is, then do it. Let me give you two more examples of extreme dedication and focus in motor racing: Nigel Mansell and Adrian Newey.

First, a little personal history. After working my way through the various feeder series such as Formula 3000, I had finally secured a test driver slot with Williams F1 in 1992. This was a massive opportunity. Not only were the team winning races – in 1992 Nigel Mansell became World Champion in the all-conquering Williams FW14B – but over the next three years I was surrounded by some of the most legendary drivers in the sport, as well as names such as Frank Williams, Patrick Head and Adrian Newey. For a lad in his early twenties, this was incredible. I had worked hard for that chance and when it came, I was ready. In terms of a learning curve, it was a staggering experience.

As part of that team, I was very lucky to work with three world champions: Nigel Mansell, Alain Prost and Ayrton Senna. In 1992 as the new test driver I didn't really have much to do with Nigel Mansell because I was just the young guy and he was the established world champion, but it didn't take me long to be around him and notice that, not surprisingly, he was very focused (like champions are) and hard working. What a lot of people didn't see was how much work Nigel also did spending time with youngsters away from the factory or track, helping kids who were less fortunate. This also extended to helping and advising young karters coming through the ranks. In my museum, there is a letter that Nigel kindly sent to my sister, generously encouraging her own karting endeavours.

I would say Nigel was not as strategic as Prost or Senna away from the circuit, which is not necessarily a criticism, but no one doubted how fast he was. Nigel was always respected for his speed.

Some people have that little extra and Nigel, especially for his bigger frame, had total commitment and bravery. He was a very courageous driver in a time when Formula 1 was an extremely dangerous sport. If he made his decision to go through a corner flat out, that right foot would never, *ever* lift. You can learn a lot from seeing someone like that. Do you lift off when the going gets tough or scary?

I will come back to his commitment later, but to get back to the point here, for all that natural speed and incredible bravery, Nigel backed it all up with massive amounts of hard work. He had huge focus on the job, there is no question about that and I suspect that comes from his working-class background.

Nigel worked on more than one occasion with another man whose work ethic is the stuff of F1 legend: Adrian Newey. As Chief Technical Officer of the Red Bull Racing Formula 1 team, Adrian is the most successful designer and technical leader in the sport. His cars have won no fewer than ten World Championships for Constructors with three teams – Williams, McLaren and Red Bull Racing – while six drivers have won the World Championship titles at the wheel of his car designs. A graduate in aerodynamics and astronautics from Southampton University, Newey first worked for the Fittipaldi Formula 1 team before joining the race car manufacturer March, where his designs won the 1985 and 1986 CART (Indycar) titles with Al Unser and Bobby Rahal. In

Formula 1 he achieved success with his impressive Leyton House March designs before joining the Williams team where he worked alongside technical director Patrick Head.

The 1992 World Championship-winning FW14B for Nigel was followed by later titles for Alain Prost, Damon Hill and Jacques Villeneuve, before he joined McLaren for the 1997 season. That is when I began working with him – his brilliant cars enabled Mika Häkkinen to win the title for McLaren in 1998 and 1999, with myself coming second in 2001.

Adrian has worked incredibly hard all his career. He is one of the highest paid designers of his generation because he has got an incredibly high strike rate – Adrian is as close a sure thing to a winning design as you are going to find. If you put Lewis Hamilton in your car or Ronaldo on a penalty kick, then you expect one outcome; Adrian has built that same reputation. However, Adrian didn't start off as a chief designer. He was a junior draughtsman. So, how do you get to such lofty levels? You've got to take that first step and apply your work ethic to every single step along the way, day after day, month after month, year after year. This takes patience. I think that in this modern world, a lot of people want the success immediately and they want to defer putting in the work till later. Maybe it's the nature of modern culture, everything is on tap, but that doesn't work in successful business, any more than it does in motorsport. You have to put the hard yards in. And besides, hard work never killed anyone. Well, it did, I suppose, such as the guy who collapsed from over-work, but you know what I mean.

So just like Schumacher, Hamilton and Mansell, one of the big lessons that anyone will take from working with Adrian Newey comes from observing his work ethic. When he goes into his design room, he goes there to focus, and he admits that he has developed the ability to really concentrate when he stands in front of his drawing board (yes, he still uses one…). He is absolutely focused on achieving his goals. His drawing board is his space to create car designs that break the mould and win world championships. He works seriously hard, long hours under immense pressure. He also happens to be a genius and extremely gifted, but he will be the first to say that counts for nothing if it isn't backed up with sheer graft.

Notably, like all people at the top of their field, Adrian has not let his work-rate slip. I've observed on many occasions how sometimes people become successful and their hard work fades away. This is often because they've become financially secure, they've realised many of their ambitions, so they don't feel the need to be as hungry as they were when they were younger. Bad mistake. When you start out in life and in your career, you crave success, maybe a nice car, a home, perhaps you have an appetite for an expensive watch or sneakers; it might not be material wants, perhaps it's travel, or maybe you are one of those people who only want success and achievement rather than any of the trimmings.

Regardless of your ambitions, if you are successful there will come a point when you maybe have those things – success, money, nice things around you, security – how, then, do you stay hungry? You often see very successful people hustling and selling themselves as if their pay cheque depends on it, when in reality they are way past financially secure. Why? Because they love the challenge, they retain the hunger and they will always be hard workers. How else do people who are financially secure for life get up and be busy each morning?

You see this attitude more often in self-employed people, for example; statistically they will take fewer days off with sick leave than those who work for a company. Partly that is because they can't afford to, but I also think it is also due to attitude. Their company is their own and that matters more than a day in a sick bed.

Never stop looking to make things happen. My father's Heinz Beans story is one of my favourite examples of someone doing this. Yet, there seems to be so many people who let things drift. What I am absolutely sure of is, in this modern world more than ever, you have to make opportunities happen. Waiting for the phone to ring is just not good enough. When someone says to me, 'Oh, I'm just waiting on this person to get back to me', to explain away why they haven't done what they were meant to do, I reply, 'Why don't you get off your backside and go and find them?' The same applies when someone is looking for work and says, 'I haven't heard back...' or 'Nothing has come through yet.' Chase them, find out what is the reason for the delay, knock on their door, be right at the front of their mind. For example, I once jumped on a plane and went to see one of my Mercedes contacts. He wrongly assumed that because of the effort I'd gone to that I was there to talk about a new driving contract, but in fact I just said, 'I just want to see if there is anything else I can do...'

Recognising how much you can influence your own journey versus waiting for others to make opportunities happen is absolutely key. Never lose the energy and desire to open doors yourself, to make connections, to progress an idea. It's fantastic having a brilliant concept or fantastic ambition but don't expect anyone to deliver it to you on a plate.

It's easy to read about the business of F1 and think these drivers are only racing for about two hours every other weekend, and even then only six months of the year. How can they talk about hard work? They just get chauffeured from the track to their private plane and jet off for a fortnight of sun, sea and the 'playboy lifestyle', right?

Well, no. Those two hours on the track each fortnight leaves 334 hours before the next race to pay attention to every aspect of a racing driver's life in detail, both on and off the circuit. The 'playboy' lifestyle came to an end with the professionalism that became a hallmark of the sport from the 1970s onwards. By detailing what goes on between races, I hope you will see just how professional, dedicated, relentless and driven Formula 1 drivers have to be to reach, and stay at, the very top – then maybe you can also analyse your own career and assess if you are doing the same.

So, the chequered flag falls, the race is over, party time starts. Not quite. Straight after a race, the driver is required to be weighed by the FIA, in all his gear, before being joined by one of the team's public relations staff in order to take them to the 'media pen', which is where all the television and radio broadcasters wait to get their soundbites and interviews. This assumes that you have not just finished on the podium, in which case you are first of all interviewed on the start–finish straight in front of the main grandstand before being taken to the 'green room', or holding room behind the podium, in order to prepare for the presentation ceremony.

This usually involves allowing you to towel down and dry off any perspiration, put on the appropriately branded baseball cap and, in the older days before individual watches were banned, put on whichever watch brand you happened to be associated with. Raising the winner's trophy with the right watch on your arm was worth a lot of positive PR to the watch companies concerned.

You then take part in two English-language press conferences; the first for broadcast media, which these days can mean TV, radio and digital or streaming media, typically quite a short affair. Each of the top three drivers has to provide a quote about how their race went, usually in response to two questions from the FIA-appointed moderator, while the race winner is then asked to give another quote in his native tongue. This is followed by the print media press conference, which is rather more drawn out as individual journalists can ask specific questions in order to add a little more depth to the story of the race.

For the driver stepping out of these post-race formalities, the next requirement is usually to go and meet-and-greet main sponsors, important team guests and hopefully contribute to the post-race celebrations in a meaningful way. This also means finding time to personally thank the team for its efforts over the weekend, including some quick feedback comments to the engineers and team management. If you have won the race, or your teammate has, there will be an official team photograph taken in the front of the garage: we win as a team, we lose as a team.

The technical debrief is next on the agenda, involving the drivers, race engineers, designers, senior technical team, engine supplier, representative of the tyre supplier if necessary, and anyone else who needs to be brought along in order to discuss what just happened.

With the media, sponsors and team debrief completed, it is usually time for the driver to have a quick shower – if available – before charging to the airport in order to either get home, or perhaps move on to the next venue. Being drenched in sweat, champagne or both, is unpleasant after a few hours, whether for you as the driver or anyone planning to travel with you!

Twenty years ago, when the majority of Formula 1 events were in Europe, it was commonplace to be able to fly home on the Sunday evening. Nowhere in Europe was more than a couple of hours' flying time from my home near Nice. That has changed in recent times, as two-thirds of the events are now in long-haul destinations. With many of these 'fly-away' races being back-to-back, either one or at most two weeks apart, it is more often the case that a driver will stay in his 'race' hotel for a further night or two before moving on to the next stop.

This is the point at which 'What do you do between races?' really kicks in. Having just done four or five hours of follow-up work after driving in a gruelling Grand Prix, Monday morning can often herald the start of an exceptionally busy schedule, something most fans never get to hear about, let alone witness.

Depending on where in the world the Grand Prix was held, there is often a sponsor wishing to use your physical presence in that country or region to ask you to do a piggy-back event on the Monday. This could be a meet-and-greet with the workforce at a factory, opening a retail store, or meeting local media. It could be all three. Personal appearances are usually organised by the team with the sponsor and a local event management company, and the number of hours you are required to attend is covered in your driver contract.

A 'personal appearance' can be defined as a four- to six-hour period, and the number of these which you are required to carry out during the course of a season is usually detailed in your contract. It can be an important negotiating point, since as I mentioned it is critical that the sponsors get their mileage out of the deal, while for the driver every day spent doing appearances is one day lost for training, testing or resting.

By Tuesday, you are normally doing further appearances or perhaps being required to visit the factory, especially if Sunday's race has allowed you to get back to Europe in time. Factory visits are important for a host of reasons, but perhaps the most beneficial of all is that the driver can participate in the full factory debrief. The driver has to remember that these are the folks who design, build and develop the car, along with all the other business-critical functions from finance to marketing, procurement to logistics, HR and quality control. At the end of the day, a Formula 1 team is simply a reasonably sized engineering and technology business, but as the driver you're the end user of the product and it is extremely important to share feedback with the entire team in person when you can.

While at the factory, the driver can also have post-race or pre-race meetings with the engineering team to discuss fixes to problems, upgrades to the car specification, or maybe a specific issue which requires some further face-to-face communications. Factory visits also usually prompt a bout of autograph signing, as the teams receive huge numbers of requests from sponsors, suppliers, fans, members of the team and their families, charitable organisations, and so on. I always felt that was important to do, as a small gesture can often go a long way.

Further public appearances for the team or its sponsors are likely to take place mid-week, and if you have back-to-back races then it is a case of being straight back into the next race weekend. If there is two-week gap between events, this can often seem like the ideal opportunity to have a little break, but in reality the team's commercial department will have been well ahead of you.

'Free' weekends between races can often mean doing 'that big event' the sponsor planned months ago specifically because you are not racing, including attending other races or historic motorsport events which have become increasingly popular in recent times. Going to the start of the Mille Miglia or doing a demonstration drive at the Goodwood Festival of Speed or Monaco Historique is all part of the job, but there is no denying it helps to contribute to a flat-out schedule. Further, if you are going to a new circuit, had some specific issues or maybe need to evaluate some aspect of performance, simulator time will usually appear on the horizon.

Given all of these daily commitments, it is vital that between races the driver makes the necessary time to maintain a proper training regime, usually involving cycling, running, swimming and gym work. It's essential to maintain this in order to sustain the ultra-fitness levels required and ensure stamina and strength do not diminish. It can mean an early start each day, carving out two or three hours to keep your body in shape before the next round of PR events, but it's not something you can skip. This is where the personal discipline really kicks in.

Family? Visits home can be few and far between during the season, so it often comes down to a snatched weekend here, a couple of nights there. More often than not, the only way you can meet your partner or children is to plan for them to attend a race, or join you at another event, when you can spend a little quality time together in the midst of an otherwise manic schedule. It means demanding a lot of them, as normal family life is suspended until you hang up your racing helmet and step away from the 200mph office.

Next up is preparing to travel to the next race, whereupon you are immediately launched into a fresh set of location-specific personal appearances and sponsor events, plus media activities on the Thursday afternoon when all the international media have turned up. There will also be the first pre-race weekend 'pre' briefing meeting with the team, running through all the specification changes since last time, upgrades, fixes and – hopefully – new, faster parts to try out.

By the time you step back on board the racing car on Friday morning, it can start to feel like this is the first opportunity you have had to sit down, focus and think about things since the last race. One thing is for certain: come Sunday afternoon after the race, win, lose, crash or retire, the 'playboy lifestyle' starts all over again.

So maybe this insight into what a racing driver actually does from day-to-day will reinforce my point that there are really no excuses when it comes to hard work. You know yourself if you have worked hard enough on a task, so don't kid yourself. Without hard work you will get nowhere, no matter how talented you are or how good your business idea may be. I learnt that from my parents, I've seen it in many world champions and motor-racing pioneers along the way and also in many of the top business people who I now come across in my daily life. I've said this before but it bears repeating: hard work is the foundation of any success and, without that basic quality, you will never truly succeed.

Everything you read in this book is predicated around the assumption that you have an intense work ethic. Without that, none of the advice on these pages can be used to its fullest extent, and there will be only one person to blame for that. Yourself. So roll your sleeves up and get on with it. No excuses.

CHAPTER 2
UNLEASHING PERSONAL POTENTIAL

A phrase that you very often hear in sports and business circles is 'Be the best version of yourself'. In fact, you hear it so often that it has become a cliché, just a few words that are thrown around without real intent or belief. But actually, these words are incredibly significant and, I believe, have been a key part of how I was able to compete in Formula 1 for so many years when, in my opinion, there were other drivers around me who were naturally faster or more inherently talented.

So let's drill down into what those words actually mean. The levels to which elite sportspeople go to achieve the very best from their own potential is exhausting and quite shocking. How do you go about becoming the best version of yourself? There are several core elements to analyse here. Firstly, before you start anything, you need a personal strategy. I will come to the importance of strategy in teamwork later but, for now, I want to stress how incredibly vital it is that you have a clear vision of your own personal goals.

Using myself as an example, you might be shocked to hear that it is no surprise I ended up in Formula 1; it is no surprise I live in Monaco; it is no surprise I work in television – because all these goals were discussed long before I actually achieved them. My father had a very perceptive long-term view even back when I was a lad. When I was 14, he said, 'David, when you get to Formula 1, I think you should live in Monaco because even if you are lucky your career will still only be ten years, so you've got to maximise your income during that period of racing.'

He knew there would be an end date when I was still a relatively young man and strategised about that fact. He went further than that. He talked about how James Hunt had successfully made the transition from racer to commentator and his relationship with Murray Walker, and he discussed with me the possibilities of moving into TV after retiring from racing. I remember him clearly saying, 'Think about that, Jackie Stewart did the same [working for American broadcasters ABC and NBC], you should consider that route, David.' Remember: I was just 14. Father was right, of course. So, almost everything that's happened so far in my life has not been a surprise. Why should you be surprised if you get to your destination when you typed in the address? If you have a vision of where you want to be, why should it surprise you when you get there?

However, just having a personal strategy isn't enough. Obviously, you can't have a vision of where you want to be and then go home, sit on the sofa and watch box sets. The doorbell won't ring itself. Opportunity does not come knocking all of its own accord. So marry the vision to a determination to succeed and deliver that through a strict work ethic.

I know some people who use what is known as vision boards, where they put images of their ambitions on a wall and look at those collages, then visualise what those ambitions will feel like and really begin to believe their goals. I don't personally do that – that's not to say I doubt the method, I just don't do it myself. However, subconsciously I guess I do practise something similar. The point is, without a clear idea of where you are heading, how on earth are you going to get there?

Secondly, in terms of beginning to unleash your personal potential, you need to know yourself and your own methods. By that I mean you need to know how you like to operate. For example, I know public speakers who plan a talk months in advance and go over their script again and again for weeks beforehand. I can't work like that. If I rehearsed weeks before, I'd just forget by the time it came to the speech. I need a certain amount of pressure to focus my mind and when that deadline approaches I find I can retain the information best and deliver it fresh and sharp at the event. That seems to keep my talks fluent and energised, it's just how I have learnt I perform better. That's not saying my method is better than someone else's, I am just saying that is how these things work *for me.*

I am aware of that and so I work with it. So by all means read up and listen to how other people perform a certain task or skill but also be aware that you may have your own method that works best for you.

Once you feel aware of your best working methods and have your strategy and plan, you need to be absolutely *committed*. Just like the effort you put in, people have different levels of what they perceive to be commitment. Here is one definition: in my late teens I'd progressed from karting into single-seater racing, starting with Formula Ford in 1989. Instead of going with one of the big established teams down south, we went with the late David Leslie who was based in Carlisle, a one-hour drive from where we lived. David was very well known and respected in racing. (His son, David Junior, was a successful sports car driver who sadly lost his life in a plane crash.)

During my time in that series, I made good progress and even started to attract a few snippets of press in magazines such as *Autosport* and *Motoring News*. The mileage to and from races was still exhausting, the standards on track were very high and I had the whole issue of learning to drive a new style of car. Single-seaters were very different from the karts I was used to. However, through applying myself to learning as fast as possible, I did quite well and managed to win the *Autosport* magazine 'Young Driver of the Year' award, which came with a test in a McLaren F1 car as part of the prize package. My career seemed to be moving along very well and we were particularly proud as we had effectively been racing with our own little family team. Then the most amazing thing happened.

At the end of my season in Formula Ford, the phone rang in my father's garage and who should it be but Jackie Stewart on the other end of the line? At first, I thought it was my mates winding me up. One of Formula 1's legendary stars, Dunbartonshire-born Jackie took to car racing as a result of being allowed to drive some fairly exotic machinery in his family's Austin and Jaguar car dealership! Initially, it looked as though his sporting triumphs might come from clay pigeon shooting; he was a crack shot, winning championships across the British Isles and Europe as a young teenager and even competing for a place in the 1960 Olympic Games. It was clear that whatever Jackie applied himself to, he did it with precision and absolute attention to detail.

Jackie initially raced in sports cars with considerable success during the early 1960s before progressing to single-seater racing first in Formula 3 then in F1. He won his first Grand Prix in his first season of World Championship Formula 1 racing. He would win three world titles before retiring in 1973 at the relatively young age of 34, but not before having established himself as one of the greatest motor-racing drivers of all time. He was moved to retire in part by his concerns for the safety of the sport he loved – he and his wife Helen lost many close friends while racing. Indeed, his retirement came on the eve of his 100th Grand Prix at Watkins Glen in the

USA in 1973, when his teammate and friend François Cevert died as the result of a horrific accident.

It comes as no surprise, therefore, that ever since hanging up his helmet, Jackie has been a leading advocate of driver safety and his unending passion to make the sport safer has seen multiple life-saving innovations used across Formula 1 and then also adopted by other motorsports.

For me, a young, aspiring Scottish driver, Jackie Stewart was one of the most influential and iconic racing drivers in the world. To have him phoning my father's garage was completely surreal. Like I said, I thought it was my mates winding me up but no, it was the three-time world champion, asking after me with regards to his three-tier race team, Paul Stewart Racing, or PSR. Jackie promptly invited me out to Switzerland to meet and talk about driving for him. He had christened the team set-up as his 'Staircase of Talent', so this was a hugely prestigious and significant moment for me. Better still, the contract with PSR was a free drive, so I did not even have to provide race funds. I moved down to Milton Keynes and spent the next three years racing with PSR, living in various rented rooms alongside mechanics and racing staff. The rented rooms were around £50 a week and could be pretty basic but I didn't care, I wasn't after luxury, I was after the chance to go racing. I didn't need a big room. What I needed was track time, a racing car and an opportunity. All the time my father and I were scraping together what extra money we could to help fund my racing as even without paying the team, racing costs a significant sum to participate. My commitment at this point was absolute: I lived, breathed and slept racing. I was very focused.

The first season of racing for PSR went reasonably well with two race wins and a season ending fourth and fifth placing in the two series I was competing in. I did break my leg at Spa, but nonetheless there was a sense of moving forward and progressing. However, after competing in Formula 3 in 1991 where I narrowly finished second in the championship, the PSR team now needed me to start contributing financially for the step up to Formula 3000, the last category before Formula 1. By this point, through a combination of various little sponsorship deals, some savings and also a very generous gift from Nana Coulthard, I had accumulated £30,000 in the bank. That was a lot of money to me aged 20, and at that time in my career, a significant financial cushion.

So when it was made known to me that in order to continue racing in Formula 3000, I needed to make a contribution to the racing costs for the season, I went to the bank, withdrew almost every penny of that £30,000 and handed it over to PSR. On that one morning, my bank balance went from £30,200 to just £200.

If you've got some financial reserve and you are not prepared to put that in to a project, yet you are asking others to do so, are you really committed? How committed are you to the potential risk and reward? Commitment is like deciding to have a baby. You can't be a wee bit pregnant, you're either in or you're not. You cannot fake commitment, at least not over a long-term period. In Formula 1, if you are not committed, they will sniff you out in days. To maximise your personal potential, you need to stay committed for years, and relentlessly so.

A good example of someone I have learnt about commitment from is Sir Frank Williams. Frank came up the hard way. Born in South Shields in the north-east of England in 1942, he started with nothing, but became a straight-talking, energetic entrepreneur. His early career as a Formula 1 entrant was arguably more notable for its failures than success, but his obsessive drive to win ultimately led to the creation of one of the most successful teams in the history of the sport. Having first entered the sport under the name Frank Williams Racing Cars in 1966, Williams endured a number of struggles until he sold the team to the Canadian oil magnate Walter Wolf ten years later. All the time, Frank's commitment and passion was turning heads. He quickly became uncomfortable working for someone else and so in 1977 he set up the Williams Grand Prix Engineering team along with his partner Patrick Head.

Frank never looked back. The team's first victory came at the 1979 British Grand Prix, when Swiss driver Clay Regazzoni took a famous win, while Frank's ambition to win the Formula 1 World Championship was realised in 1980 with Australia's Alan Jones winning the Driver's title and the team tying up the Constructor's series. Williams followed that with a second title in 1982, this time with Keke Rosberg. More titles would follow with Nelson Piquet (1987), Nigel Mansell (1992), Alain Prost (1993), Damon Hill (1996) and Jacques Villeneuve (1997). The team has won a total of seven Drivers and nine Constructors World Championships, winning 114 Grands Prix along the way.

Frank Williams' commitment and drive to be the very best he could be is legendary. This commitment and passion was never more apparent than during a very serious and harrowing event in Frank's private life. In 1986, Frank suffered a serious spinal injury as the result of a road accident in France, leaving him tetraplegic. Until then he had been a competitive middle-distance runner; after such a terrible accident, most people – nearly all, surely? – would have caved in, retreated to a quieter life, pared back their ambition.

Not Frank Williams. That's not how he operates and that is why, when you are around him, you can feed off that famous commitment and passion. Incredibly, his high levels of physical fitness at the time of the accident, combined with his huge work ethic, determination and fortitude in the face of adversity, saw him return to running the Williams team full-time within a few months. Frank remains at the head of the team to this day, a giant of the sport, knighted by the Queen in 1999 and also awarded France's prestigious Legion d'Honneur. Frank's remarkable life story should, in itself, be all you need to know about commitment.

As I mentioned earlier, my part in the Williams F1 story came in the early 1990s. It was Frank who would recognise my own commitment as an up-and-coming young racer and offer me a role as a test driver for Williams in 1992, my first opportunity in Formula 1; it was Frank who would then offer me a full race seat in the aftermath of Ayrton Senna's tragic death in 1994. Having had the great fortune to race for Frank and Williams F1 no less than 25 times from 1994 through all of 1995, there were many micro-examples along the way of his personal commitment. As much as he is fiercely committed, he also expects the same of the people in his team. He leads by example and he expects that example to be followed.

One day when I was quite new to the team, I was in the office and the conversation was centred around the extreme level of fitness required to successfully drive a Formula 1 car. Every driver at that level is very fit but given Frank's own athletics background and impressive fitness, he saw it as a given that his drivers would be supremely fit. The idea of his drivers not being as fit as Bruce Lee, at the very top end of athletic prowess, was totally unacceptable to him. At this point, Frank asked to see my abs, simply as a very stark indication of whether I had the necessary level of super-fitness. If you can't apply yourself to being super-fit when someone is offering you an F1 drive, then what does that say about your level of commitment? And the point is that Frank knew abs can't be cheated, you have either put in the hard yards or you haven't, so he knew that that simple physical sign was a key indicator of a driver's level of commitment.

Fortunately, due to my own punishing fitness regime, my abs were very clear for all to see, the result of hours and hours keeping super-fit. That level of fitness is in itself an example of my commitment to racing and my drive to maximise my own personal potential. I am a tall man to be racing cars. Some of the modern drivers are really quite short, because there is an obvious weight-to-performance correlation. You might wonder how such relatively small amounts of weight can make such a difference in a race car. Well, each additional kilogram of weight in a car will cost around 0.035 seconds per lap on an average circuit. This is one reason why Mark Webber, who was around five kilos heavier than Seb Vettel, due to a significant height difference, could expect to be up to 0.175 seconds slower. This advantage is reinforced by the fact that a lighter driver means the team can ideally locate ballast in order to bring the combined car/driver up to the minimum weight requirement. In so doing, you can actually improve vehicle performance, tyre wear and handling. So you can see that driver weight is absolutely crucial and you can also see why Sir Frank – or indeed any other team manager – would question a driver's commitment if he turned up for pre-season testing looking overweight. If the team and their designers had made significant improvements in the off-season, only for a driver to turn up overweight and cost them fractions of seconds every lap, how is that helpful? If you can identify areas where you can influence the outcome, why would you not do that? In my opinion, the answer to these questions is a lack of commitment. In turn, this means you are not maximising your own personal potential.

In the past I've joked that I was a normally tall man in a paddock full of mini-men. For such a tall race driver, I had to go the extra mile for years to compete on a level playing field. This started way back when I was karting. I was always very keen to be extremely fit. We had a few exercise machines at home that I used, as well as free weights and so on. We were also lucky enough to eventually get a pool at home so I would do lap after lap in there, too. I even used to do some exercises with a helmet on with lead weights strapped to the side, to strengthen my neck in a very specific way. I watched my diet carefully; back then I was six foot tall but weighed just over nine stone. Even then, I was running heavy in the kart. However, my commitment and drive to win began to extend to trains of thought that I would absolutely not recommend to young drivers, because this obsessive edge to maintain my weight and fitness eventually slipped into bulimia. Around the age of 16, I would make myself vomit to maintain weight control. I weighed myself three times a day. If I was half a pound heavier, I'd do some laps in the pool. That got rid of the weight but it was clearly not a healthy way to control my size and cannot be condoned. It was more a reflection of my absolute determination to succeed. The

way I looked at it, if I could influence my race that way, then
why would I not do that? I would never endorse going to those
extremes, of course. Nonetheless, I do see race drivers who are
bigger lads (as in carrying weight, rather than being tall) and I just
think, *How committed are you if you can't control your weight to an ideal
level for the team?* By that, I don't mean for a second they should
be as extreme as I was. What I am suggesting is that if your team
says the car will be faster if you weigh 70 kilos, then you should do
what you can to get to 70 kilos.

What that meant for me was that for my entire racing career I
had to control my weight very carefully. Once I progressed into the
lower single-seater series and ultimately Formula 1, I did this through
eating very healthily and exercising to a strict and at times punishing
regime. I had trainers and people to help me do that carefully, but
I still had to put the work in. Having the right nutrition is key,
which is why the champagne offered at the sponsor reception, or
the five-course gala dinner, often went unconsumed. I literally could
not eat or drink whatever was put in front of me. A race-weight of
around 70 kilos is low for a six-foot man, so maintaining that was
always a challenge. Alcohol is out, unless you can sneak a (small)
celebratory glass after a good result on Sunday, and your well-being
is further enhanced by ensuring that you get enough sleep. With
so much long-haul travel this can be difficult, but working on the
right balance of training, nutrition and sleep is critical if you want

to maintain the energy levels from race to race. This was all pretty demanding but I had no problem with that.

Jackie Stewart was one of the first people to tip me off to understanding diet and fitness. Until I was 19, I used to have a cooked breakfast on a Sunday, and then Jackie said, 'You need to eat healthily and started having muesli.' Bear in mind Jackie was racing many years before most drivers were looking into diet and that level of detail. Even in that regard, Jackie was well ahead of the pack.

Another example of being committed and therefore maximising my own ability would be testing. I looked at every time in the car as a rehearsal because eventually you are no longer rehearsing and you are in fact at a live race event. I put my heart and soul into every test lap. I actually had bigger crashes in testing than I ever did in Grand Prix racing. Driving a Grand Prix car takes enormous concentration. If you don't apply that at all times, how can you be surprised when you crash? When I went to test, I went there with absolute focus to get the most out of that day. To me that's very logical. You get out what you put in. That is heightened in F1 because even in testing, a mistake can lead to a crash, and a crash can lead to a serious injury or fatality. So there was no room, in my mind at least, to not test at 100 per cent. I would treat each corner, each practice start, each lap, all the feedback from the engineers, everything about testing, my whole entire day, as if it was a race. That way, when the race day arrived, I had already rehearsed all those tiny details. When you test, you might actually drive the equivalent of four or five Grands Prix in that time, so the concentration in that car all day is exhausting. However, you are the voice of that car, so you cannot afford to do a few laps at half-pace. You have to direct your team to the relevant data, you must test the car at full tilt, I don't see any other way to approach testing.

I'm not sure some of my peers would be able to say the same – I'm not sure Mika put as much effort into testing as he did racing but, to be fair, he clearly had the talent to deliver when it came to racing. As I said earlier, I think my commitment and work ethic is the reason why I was at McLaren for nine years, longer than any other driver in the history of the team. They knew I was committed. People could feel that commitment, they could sense that this really mattered to me. You don't need to be the best to be successful. However, you have got to be absolutely committed to your plan.

Before I move on to the next element of unleashing your personal potential, let me quickly talk about another F1 character who can teach you about commitment and who certainly did maximise his own potential, Nigel Mansell (again). Superficially Nigel Mansell, 'Our Nige', was a huge fans' favourite, thanks to his spectacular driving style and his down-to-earth persona. I've talked already about his work ethic but in terms of commitment, Mansell's relentless quest to win the World Championship against all odds is really a remarkable exercise in persistence despite repeated disappointments and challenges. He came to racing relatively late, starting in karts before winning the 1977 British Formula Ford Championship, winning 33 of 42 races. Three uncompetitive and financially very challenging seasons passed before Mansell was spotted by Colin Chapman, boss of Team Lotus, and given a test. He became Lotus's test driver, and made his Grand Prix debut at the 1980 Austrian Grand Prix, one of three Formula 1 races in which he would compete that year. He continued with Team Lotus for four full seasons before he joined Williams in 1985 and never looked back. Famously, he narrowly missed out on winning the 1986 Formula 1 World Championship when a tyre exploded while he was leading the final round of the championship in Adelaide, Australia, but this kind of spectacular failure only enhanced Mansell's reputation as an all-or-nothing racer who breathed total commitment. This was reinforced when he moved to Ferrari, taking a fairy-tale victory on his debut for the Italian team in an unreliable car at the 1989 Brazilian Grand Prix.

All the years of hard work and commitment finally paid off when he took the 1992 World Championship at precisely the moment when it seemed he might forever play the part of bridesmaid; he made that final step to domination that year, taking nine victories in the brilliant Williams-Renault FW14B. Contractual difficulties saw him migrate to the USA where, again against all the odds and due in large part to his level of commitment and determination to win, he became the only driver ever to win the CART (Championship Auto Racing Teams) series while still F1 World Champion.

If you are talking about commitment, you also need to look at Mansell's injuries, suffered in an era when drivers were still being crippled and killed too frequently. He suffered a broken neck in a Formula Ford accident and broken vertebrae after an enormous crash in Formula 3. He suffered severe fuel burns on his Grand Prix debut for Team Lotus, a colossal 200mph accident during practice for the 1985 French Grand Prix, and another spinal injury during a high-speed qualifying accident in Japan in 1987. After a near-200mph crash into a concrete wall in CART at Phoenix, his injuries were so severe that the only person able to analyse what he had suffered was an aerospace pathologist, who stated the sole time he had seen such severe damage to the back before was in plane crash fatalities – as a result the injury was renamed 'The Mansell Lesion'. Yet he somehow managed to get back in a car two weeks later, put the car on pole and eventually finish third. That is commitment.

• • •

Going back to the moment Frank expected to see my perfectly toned and ripped abs, not only was that an indication of the commitment he expected, but it also helps to illustrate my next point about maximising your own personal potential by *making yourself indispensable*. After that incident, I knew the type of driver Frank wanted to see in one of his cars. The point being, you need to educate yourself on what the boss expects and wants. That way, he or she will think, *Okay, this person's committed*, which therefore makes it difficult for them to not 'have you in the car'.

If you create the best version of yourself and that becomes indispensable to the team or company, then you are likely to be a success; if your best version is still not good enough, then at least you know the areas to work on improving. As a Formula 1 driver, if you don't maximise your personal potential, then you will quickly fall by the wayside. Think about the scale of the employment opportunities for any F1 driver: there are millions and millions of people around the world who can drive, yet there are only 20 people at any given time who are out there in a Grand Prix car. If you are not making yourself indispensable, your employers will quickly find someone to replace you.

In F1, this precarious position is acute. As drivers, we are absolutely in tune with the fact that we sign a beautiful marriage contract for one year, two years, maybe three years but on the same day we sign that contract, the divorce papers are ready because it *will* come to an end. Even with McLaren, where I was considered to be a relatively long-term fixture, I was only there nine years. (Perhaps a more extreme example of this is in football where the average tenure for managers is often measured in months not years.) I was acutely aware of this fragile employment security the day I first signed to Williams to start my F1 career, and every season after that I determined to make myself indispensable, so that the marriage with whichever team I was involved would last as long as possible.

In my opinion, there are two ways to make yourself indispensable. The first way is not something I approve of – it's when people 'keep the keys' to everything. By that I mean they keep all the knowledge close to their chest, they hide trade secrets, if you like, their logic being that this makes them a necessity for the business. That may be the case but this approach is a negative, selfish and unhelpful strategy, with no thought or consideration about the benefits to the team.

People hold back information because that is perceived as retaining power. I strongly disagree with this – by sharp contrast I am a great believer in *sharing* information. A small example is that I'm a great believer that everyone is copied into an email. Some people often say, 'Well, he doesn't need that information, why is he copied in?' Well, an email is not like someone phoning you or knocking on your door. It doesn't disturb you. The information might not directly relate to someone but at least they know where the process is heading. Why is that a problem? And that person might even have something to add. In any process, in any business, you are building something and everyone has got to know when they are required and what is their responsibility, which is why I am a huge advocate of sharing rather than withholding information. I cannot emphasise enough just how important it is to collaborate and accept that it is by sharing knowledge and working together as a team, we inevitably end up in a better place.

Therefore, the second way to make yourself indispensable is far better, more honourable and, I believe, superior in every way: trust in the power of everyone coming together to improve the team or the business. This requires confidence in your own ability, of course.

However, by taking the second approach to making yourself indispensable, you do have to acknowledge that there is an inherent risk that you may improve the business in some way that ultimately makes you very much dispensable.

Case in point: myself and Sebastian Vettel.

In top-level sport you realise your career is probably around 10 to 15 years long, after which time you would be somewhat deluded not to recognise that opportunities may start to diminish. By working with everyone for the benefit of the team, there is always that chance that you are eventually writing yourself out of a job and that is what happened with Sebastian Vettel.

At the beginning of 2008, I was testing for Red Bull Racing in Barcelona when I tweaked my neck driving over a kerb which left me with limited movement and in need of physio. Seb Vettel was there driving for Toro Rosso, so I suggested to team principal Christian Horner to get Seb in the car because he'd done a very good job at Sauber in a one-off race and had certainly earned the Toro Rosso drive; to me he was clearly very good, so I made that suggestion and that led to his going in my car that day. Remember, Sebastian was this young, up-and-coming driver and by letting him get in my car to show everyone what he was capable of, I was risking writing myself out of a drive. I remember my contracts manager at the time Martin Brundle saying that it was like a turkey voting for Christmas. I saw it a different way. I knew that the 2008 season was my 37th year, and more than likely to be my last, so why swim against the tide? Martin thought that was a bad decision and I understand his position on that, although I disagreed. I thought it was good business.

So how was this good business? I was taking a long-term view and doing what I felt was right for the team. Like I said, I was aware that my racing career was heading towards closure. I was also aware that this young German driver was extremely talented and that Red Bull as a team would benefit enormously from having him signed up and in one of their cars. You may consider that a relatively selfless act in what could be seen as a very egotistical self-centred world and you would arguably be right. Formula 1 is often seen as a very ruthless sport and it certainly can be, but one aspect of that world that should be replicated by business is F1's eagerness to hold on to expertise and keep it within the paddock. Yes, F1 has to be about the new, young drivers on the grid, they are the lifeblood and future of the sport, that is how it should be and that is why I suggested putting Seb in my car. At a certain point, it is a biological fact that age and Father Time precludes you from racing at that very top level, no matter how astonishing your skills are. However, I knew that in Formula 1 it is very often the case that when a driver retires, he is frequently moved into another role. Crucially, unlike some businesses, it is not seen as a demotion, it is a natural part of the business model and considered good practice. Why would you let a brain that has all that experience in real world events move out of your business? It makes no sense at all. So although I was no longer indispensable to Red Bull, I had proven myself worthy of being retained in the business. A decade later, at the time of writing I am still under contract to Red Bull, so to my mind that has proven to be a good decision. That would suggest that despite offering the drive to Sebastian rather than me, Red Bull still felt I was indispensable to their wider ambitions. I had recognised that my role was more than just looking out for myself and that I had a part to play in growing and advancing the team. To be honest, I probably did not realise just how good Seb would turn out to be; however, it is nice to think that I played a small part in helping Red Bull to accelerate Sebastian's own career and maximum performance and, in turn, I helped the team unleash its own potential.

There was a risk, of course. There are parallels in F1 where teams have taken good advice or opportunities forwarded by drivers and not reciprocated. But I trusted Red Bull, I trusted in the team and the people who I had come to work alongside and, sure enough, they did reciprocate. I didn't know they would for certain, but recommending

Sebastian was the right thing to do. Listen, I'm not trying to pretend to be Mother Teresa, but equally when the writing is on the wall or you see someone that is young and up-and-coming with their entire career ahead of them, recognise that moment and think about the team. It felt right. It felt selfless, it felt like we – as a team – would benefit from that suggestion to put Sebastian in the car that day.

· · ·

The next way to unleash your personal potential is to never stop learning. Formula 1 is a sport that is on a constant learning curve. I've been lucky enough to spend many years around some incredible minds and, because I'm always thirsty for knowledge, their guidance has been pivotal. Initially, that learning curve was from my parents and the way they worked with customers and clients; as an adult I've had further guidance and learnt so much from a number of key individuals. That hunger for learning is still very much alive in me, I feel that need to learn every single day.

In Formula 1 you have many more failures than you have success. Even the mighty Michael Schumacher 'only' won 91 Grands Prix after starting in 301. However, the great thing about that environment is that we enjoy learning and improving. It is a constant process of reviewing performance, looking at the gaps, and being honest about our mistakes. This means being prepared to talk about what did not work as well as what did work, and aiming to be better next time out. Formula 1 does this in so many ways, which

I will expand on in later chapters, but for now a simple illustration would be every day at the race track, whether testing or racing, we have a morning meeting with the relevant engineers and team leaders in order to discuss what our plans are for the day ahead, and then this will be followed up by another meeting at the end of that day in order to review how we had performed against the plan. That creates a culture of constant learning, and continuous improvement.

Another way to keep constantly learning is to regularly challenge yourself to achieve ambitious goals. People who are successful in the long term are always learning, they don't rest on their laurels, they don't assume they know everything about their business, they approach every situation and think, *What can I learn from this event or this person?* To be challenged in life brings out the best version of yourself. People either rise to the challenge or meander through life avoiding them. I think a life well lived is one that is constantly being educated and putting yourself into environments that are outside your comfort zone – that way you will learn, and you will use your social and life skills to adapt and to evolve. To stay within the safety of a familiar world is understandable to a degree, but at a certain point that becomes very limiting and you will not evolve and develop your skills which will then curtail your learning. This will inevitably limit your business potential.

Perhaps I like to challenge myself more than most because my life in racing was perceived, by some at least, as risky. As I will explain later in this book, I didn't see it like that, but what I will admit to is that being a professional racing driver does constantly present you with challenges. That might be a parts failure, a driver going round a certain corner more quickly than you, team politics, all sorts of issues. All challenges to be faced and overcome. I love facing challenges because I know that on the other side I will be a better racer, businessman or person.

I remember back in my days racing Formula Ford, I was out on track testing at Silverstone in this fairly quick single-seater when suddenly, out of nowhere, this Formula 3000 car went past me like a rocket. It was literally a blur, I was staggered. I just remember thinking, *How the hell is he able to drive that fast?* That was Formula 3000; Formula 1 was another significant step faster and yet the latter was my ultimate goal. I just sat there thinking, *How can I possibly get that fast?* That is a challenge.

Inevitably, if you are challenging yourself, you will encounter situations where you don't know the answer, or maybe don't know a certain technique or piece of information. If that happens, *just ask*. My view is, if I don't know, I will find someone who does and engage with them because that is what you do as a team. Who is the best person for that job, who do I know who can deliver that for me? People can carry too much ego into their careers, they become afraid to ask in case it shows a perceived weakness or inferiority. That's nonsense. If you don't know something, say you don't know and, crucially, don't be embarrassed by not knowing. In F1, if people don't know something and they try and wing it and just bullshit, they get found out *very* quickly. If you've been a successful sportsperson, then likely you are aware of the benefits of taking on board other people's opinions, 'Ah, so, I've just learnt something.'

I'm never frightened to ask a question about something I don't know or an issue that I think might be done better another way. For example, with my work in TV, I wouldn't know how to even switch on an editing machine but it doesn't mean that I don't have a view on what a certain part of a programme could look like – and I've got no hang up or embarrassment about asking why are we doing it a certain way. It doesn't need to be confrontational and if you think about this, it's a win–win. If they explain what they are doing and agree it could be improved with your idea then that's a plus; if they explain and you realise why their original plan is the best way, then you've learnt something, you've been educated. If you think you can't learn something from someone else, your mindset is probably stopping you from getting the best out of life's opportunities. You can apply this to whatever sport or career you are involved in. It shouldn't be about a fear of failure, it is about a desire for success.

If you only ever work with people who agree with you all the time, then how is that going to keep you growing and evolving? Take Ron Dennis. Now, he is well known for having some very strong opinions. Not everyone agrees with him. However, contrary to what you might think, he is absolutely able to accept different opinions. For example, when I published my autobiography in 2007, Ron Dennis wrote a very eloquent and complimentary foreword for my book. This surprised many people because some sections of my first book were less than complimentary about certain aspects of my time at McLaren. In particular, I explained that at times I felt Ron had favoured Mika Häkkinen and how the consequence of this on my confidence was rather toxic and destructive. Despite this, in his foreword, Ron very magnanimously apologised if I 'sometimes felt a little unloved at McLaren'. He also said, 'I do not necessarily agree with everything David has written on the pages that follow, but in a sense it does not matter.' For my part, when I wrote that book, part of me felt guilty for not saying exclusively positive things about McLaren and Ron, because they gave me the opportunity to race at the very front of the grid. However, I voiced my opinion respectfully and clearly and Ron accepted that and did the same in return; like me, he didn't agree, but he accepted our differing views.

There are hundreds of examples in F1 of people who voice strong opinions; it is not a sport for the shrinking violet. Lewis Hamilton is not ashamed to voice an opinion because he believes in his talent and has a wealth of experience to back that up. With so much success, his team have to listen to him. However, from my time at McLaren, I know that way back when he was a junior, he still voiced an opinion in a constructive manner. Bernie Ecclestone is another perfect example of someone who can gracefully and skilfully express strong opinions. What he achieved for Formula 1 is remarkable – he somehow managed to grow and grow the sport for many years, all the time dealing with all sorts of very powerful and super-confident individuals, all with their own strongly held views. Yet he was always able to listen and make them feel a part of the conversation.

Part of the skill in Formula 1 is people's ability to discuss rather than argue. There is a crucial difference. If F1 people just argued all the time, nothing would ever get done because there are, frankly, so many things to fall out about! Seriously, though, whatever field you are in, learning how accept different points of view while still making your own argument articulately and without confrontation is crucial. It's quite clever how different people approach this challenge. One of the most graceful is Gerhard Berger; whenever he has a different view from you, he uses the expression, 'I see it another way'. Brilliantly non-confrontational.

Naturally, I have not always been involved in such graceful discussion. During my time at McLaren, alongside my teammate Mika Häkkinen we battled for several seasons against the might of Ferrari and Michael Schumacher at the peak of their powers. We did not always manage to beat Michael, but I think we gave him plenty of competition. However, on one occasion I certainly caused him to be upset with me when we collided at the Belgian Grand Prix.

As the result of having started in the spare car after an early pile-up had caused a restart, I was a lap behind leader Michael after just 24 laps. On lap 25, in poor weather conditions, Schumacher came up to lap me and felt he was being held up. He radioed the Ferrari team whose boss, Jean Todt, then went and spoke to the McLaren team to ensure that I would move out of the way. I duly slowed to let Michael pass at Pouhon corner, but he was unsighted in the spray and ran straight into the back of my McLaren. The collision ripped a wheel off the Ferrari, causing Schumacher to retire from the race; he blamed me for intentionally blocking him and causing the accident. Not only did the collision cost Schumacher the win, but it handed victory to Damon Hill who then won the race for Jordan. Michael was not a happy man. He stormed into our garage looking very angry. That was one occasion when my racing helmet stayed firmly on my head. I am a lot braver inside the car than outside!

On a more serious note, learning to express an opinion articulately and calmly while taking on board other people's opinions without turning events into an argument is a vital skill you need to learn to unleash your personal potential. A related idea that is a crucial part of your campaign to achieve this is the notion that you should be conscious of who you are mixing with. Not in some snobbish or prejudiced way, but in terms of the fact that you will often be judged not only on your own performance but by those you hang around with. For example, I will not be around mean people, either financially or in terms of their personality. People who are mean are just atmosphere vacuums. They are horrible to be around. You need to surround yourself with positive energy and positive people; mean and negative people just drain the energy away from you. I think it was Jackie that told me the expression, 'If you fly with the crows, you'll be shot at.' Now, although I don't know why people would shoot crows, I guess that is his way of saying, 'Be aware of the company you keep'.

Of course, with so many opinions and decisions to be made in sport and in business, sometimes you will make mistakes. Everyone does. If you are to learn and maximise your potential, it is vital that when this happens you acknowledge your own error. It amazes me how many people in business – and in life – cannot do this simple thing.

I learnt the importance of admitting mistakes very young. When I was karting, a fantastic chap called Dave Boyce was a central part of the team and I learnt a lot from him. When I first met him he was already running future multiple Le Mans winner Allan McNish and had a renowned reputation in karting. He always said I was the most particular of his karters, so if he changed the set-up slightly, I would know and ask him why! Dave Boyce taught me to admit mistakes – and that it is a good habit to get into. If I made an error on track, he would encourage me to say why, point out where and we could then discuss and learn from that. What is the point of hiding and pretending no mistake has been made? How can you learn from that? Recently, he has been helping our son with his own karting and I see it there, too. I will often see Dave at the track calling my lad over and saying, 'What were you doing over there?' The first time it happened, my son came over to me with a tear in his eyes, saying, 'He shouted at me', but I explained that Dave wasn't shouting, he was guiding, he was helping.

In F1 we tend to be very responsibility driven. The responsibility culture of motorsport and sport in general is something that I think is really impressive. We aim to avoid a blame culture. We individually take responsibility for our particular roles because any errors or oversights will get found out anyway – if you really care about your team why would you want to hide that and not admit your mistake?

Sometimes of course you can't really hide the error anyway! Lewis Hamilton famously pulled into the McLaren garage at the 2013 Malaysian Grand Prix for a pit stop even though he had recently left that team and gone to drive for Mercedes. Force of habit, maybe, but that proved to be a critical personal error that cost his team time – although the Red Bulls were dominant that weekend and he was not going to win anyway, his third place was still compromised by around four to five seconds by that slip-up. (Every time I watch the clip of that pit stop, I wonder what would've happened if the McLaren mechanics had simply taken his wheels off and walked slowly away!) When something like this goes wrong,

Formula 1 turns the event into a positive experience because the team sits down, looks at what happened, modifies the process if needed, and makes sure they do not have a repeat occurrence in the future. They can only do this if people calmly admit their mistakes and take responsibility for them.

Good race drivers are the first to hold their hands up and admit an error. 'Yes, my mistake, sorry, won't do it again.' Pretty simple words to say, it just seems it's hard for some people to say them. I think in a lot of businesses, people can hide from responsibility, which doesn't help at all. It shifts blame to someone else usually, and that may or may not be justified, but either way it isn't solving the problem.

At Williams, I suffered an accident not long after I took my race seat after the tragic death of Ayrton Senna. At the time, it was inevitable that any accidents in a Williams car would be highly scrutinised. My incident turned out to be due to my steering failing, unfortunately because one of the mechanics had forgotten to tighten a nut correctly so it basically fell out – that wasn't a good moment for me, especially as I suffered a minor concussion. The team owner, Frank Williams, came directly to Silverstone race track to see me and brought in the mechanic who hadn't done his job properly; it would have been easy to be upset and ask Frank to sack him, but the reality was that the mechanic was himself devastated by what had happened. As a result, we could see that he would never make such a mistake again. The people who make the mistakes can often be the most useful people for us to learn from about how to improve the process so that the problem never reoccurs. So if you make a mistake, admit it, discuss it and then learn from it. Your potential will be increased as a result.

· · ·

So unleashing your personal potential can be achieved by knowing your methods, being totally committed, making yourself indispensable, never being afraid to ask, always remaining hungry to learn, being able to discuss calmly and always admitting your mistakes so that you can learn even more. Inevitably, however, there will be times when things don't work out – when, for some reason, despite all your best intentions and hard work, a project fails or underachieves… when you *lose*. What do you do then? Well, rather than being a knock-back, these moments are actually the most fantastic opportunities to increase your personal capabilities even more!

In sport, especially in the business of F1, you lose more than you win. In fact, I can take it further than that. In top-level sport you will eventually be replaced; it's inevitable. In that sense, if someone else takes your drive (in effect, they win the contract you wanted), then they have won that particular battle and you have lost. It is a simple and unavoidable fact of life that teams and companies have to make the best decisions for who is the right person for the job based on their needs, so the only way to avoid ever being in that position is to make yourself the boss – if you cannot handle rejection, then maybe you have to be self-employed. However, if that is not for you, then realising the point when you are no longer the primary choice has to be dealt with and reacted to, so that it becomes a productive moment rather than a negative one.

In my view, when you lose, you either become a victim or you attack, and I don't like to be a victim. This happened to me at McLaren – I have already mentioned that in F1 you sign a marriage contract but as you do you are fully aware that divorce is inevitable. Well, my marriage to McLaren ended at the Brazilian Grand Prix in 2004; it was a disappointing race, with a tricky spell out on slicks in drizzling rain and an 11th place finish. I had known for some time that McLaren was going to sign the Colombian Juan Pablo Montoya for the following season, and I felt it was unlikely that this new driver would replace my then-teammate, Kimi Räikkönen, so it looked like my time was up. As an aside, although I knew in private, McLaren chose the moment to publically announce that Montoya was replacing me while I was on holiday… with Ron Dennis… on a yacht. Awkward!

The record books show that Montoya only lasted a season and a half at McLaren (I'd been there nine years), and his performances were inferior to mine. So I believe that McLaren made the wrong choice. However, that is irrelevant – they did what they thought was best for the team, which is their absolute prerogative and it served no purpose whatsoever for me to dwell on that. Another driver had the contract I'd wanted, so I had to face up to that and move forward.

The stark facts were that when I crossed the finish line in Brazil that year, I left the paddock with no drive for the following year. My racing career appeared to be over.

So what did I do?

I went back to basics. I phoned Ferrari, Williams and Renault and said, 'I will be your test driver.' Jean Todt at Ferrari and Flavio Briatore at Renault both said, 'We've got two test drivers and don't feel comfortable offering you the third test driver slot out of respect for your career.' Patrick Head at Williams said, 'Are you sure you are really committed to being a test driver?' and I said, 'Yes, absolutely. I believe that I will show you I still have the speed and the commitment.' Like I've said, it's all about believing in yourself and showing people that you believe in yourself. Not in an arrogant way, but in a believable, authentic way. Unfortunately, no one had any openings as everything was contracted but they all very respectfully declined my proposal. That respect was appreciated but it didn't resolve my challenge so I kept on going – ultimately I would find a drive for Red Bull, which I will come to later.

Once you have experienced loss or failure, you are actually a very lucky person. You can use that superficially negative event to increase your personal potential. Why do I say that? Because in sport, business and life, our biggest opportunity and greatest potential come out of failure. That is when you can learn, you can move forward, you can avoid repeating the mistakes that have just occurred. This is a core reason why I encourage everyone to be involved in sports. It teaches you about success and failure. I categorically do not believe it is correct for schools to have competitions where 'no one loses'. What is the purpose of that? What is it teaching the children? I get that they are trying to protect kids from being upset, but in the real world when they are grown-ups, if they pitch for a contract, the client won't say, 'You've all done super-well, no one is the winner, no one is the loser.' I accept that a psychologist or a more intelligent, informed individual could explain the potential difficulties that losing at sports day might create for kids when they become adults, but I'm personally not convinced it is a good idea. I want our son to have the most full and loving life he possibly can, but I'm not prepared to tell him he is a winner when he's lost! I want him to understand we all have our skills and talents and finding where they are best deployed in life is ultimately the point of entering in the first place.

In sport, even the most phenomenally talented people don't always win. Even they have to process the experience of losing. However, this then makes them analyse their performance, what went wrong, what can be improved, what lessons can be learnt. In turn this increases their potential. If you can't handle those disappointments then you are absolutely not equipped to be either in a team or business environment.

Some people review failures or losses with a massive dose of 'What if?' That's a complete waste of time. I don't have time for 'what if'. How will you learn and therefore increase your potential by saying that? In my racing career, I lost several Grands Prix through absolutely no fault of my own, but because of a technical fault or parts failure that ended my race. When that happens, explain to me any benefit of complaining about what if, or dwelling on what might have been. 'If only I'd had seven numbers on the lottery instead of three…' Pointless. What you must do is take that failure and analyse it, find the positives, learn the lessons, increase your potential as a result. But don't talk about 'if only…' You didn't win, now you know why you didn't win, so use that information and evolve. Even with the best of intentions you don't always get the outcome you think you deserve, in business and in sport, but you have got to be able to compartmentalise that, learn from it and move on. Not 'what if?' but instead, 'Where is the next opportunity?'

I'd like to briefly make a related point about the ethics of this subject. I spent a large part of my life in a world where crossing the finish line first was a massive target, it dominated every second of every day. On 13 occasions in F1, I did exactly that, I won the Grand Prix. On all the other occasions when that didn't happen, I tried my very best to maximise my personal potential to get there first. However, that doesn't mean I would do anything to win. I would rather win in style and fairly than by cheating. Formula 1 has strict rules and regulations that have to be adhered to, but it goes without saying that some parties might see how far that can be tested. There is a legal way of doing that, for example by designing a car that exploits so-called loopholes in the rules, is fully compliant with the regulations but gives a sizeable speed advantage through some clever new innovation or design. Then there are people who will use whatever methods they can, legitimate or not. This applies to any sport, any business and in life in general, of course.

I would never want to be in the latter category. Where is the reward in victory by cheating? How is cheating unleashing your potential? I don't follow that. I think in sport and in business you have got to follow the rules. So, it's not win at any cost. I know there are those who say, 'Show me a good loser and I'll show you a loser' but I dislike that phrase intensely.

There is no shame in not winning. There is only shame in cheating.

• • •

So unleashing your personal potential, being the best you can be, creating the ultimate version of yourself, however you want to phrase it, is a crucial part of any successful sports- or business person. If I may indulge myself and use my own experiences battling with seven-time world champion Michael Schumacher by way of illustration, hopefully you can see how I personally tried to unleash my potential by drawing on all the ideas I have summarised in this chapter. I knew that unless I was the very best version of myself on track, in testing and behind the scenes, I had no chance against Michael and the

Ferraris. I was up against a man who is widely regarded as one of the all-time great drivers, arguably *the* greatest driver, who was driving ridiculously fast and reliable cars.

The only way I had a chance was to maximise my personal potential by breaking down every single element of my job and finding a way to run that aspect to its individual limit. This was no easy task. Being a Formula 1 driver is intensely demanding because, aside from having the skill to take one of these machines to the absolute limit lap after lap, it is vital to maintain your physical and mental condition so that you are able to perform to the maximum of your ability from start to finish. The physical demands range from the 5G forces you have to withstand in high-speed corners to the high ambient temperatures, which can cause you to lose two to three kilos in body weight during a Grand Prix in Malaysia, Singapore or Monte Carlo.

The physical demands are severe: there's a lot of noise, vibration, heat, vertical and lateral movement. On top of that you have to be able to process a lot of information in terms of car positioning on the race track, information being displayed on the multi-function steering wheel and audio communication with the race engineer whose job it is to help adjust tactics and strategy as the race unfolds. This is all without considering your race rivals and 19 other cars hurtling around the track at speeds of over 200mph. So it requires extreme mental alertness and extreme dexterity. If you think about it, this means that many things other than simply driving quickly become very important.

Therefore my approach to trying to beat Schumacher was that if I maximised *all of the components*, not just my driving, then I'd have a chance. So I analysed every single element that might give me an edge: I trained harder, I was in incredible physical shape; I studied the telemetry of every test and race for hours; I spoke with the engineers endlessly about the upgrades and the car set-up and gave them the best possible feedback; I analysed every track, every corner, every pit stop in minute detail; I worked with the designers to make myself as comfortable as possible in the car, to avoid any distractions during the race, and also worked hard on perfecting the ergonomics, including the location of buttons, switches and dials on the steering wheel and within the cockpit; I worked with key suppliers, such as tyres and brakes, to get the most out of them; I looked for errors I'd made and how I could remove that from my future, as well as being unafraid to be self-critical if it was needed; I analysed my teammate Mika Häkkinen's data to see where his gains or losses would be, as together we could work to cut into Michael's edge; I studied my competition, specifically Schumacher's split times, and any information we could gain by looking at his car, to understand where he was gaining time. In summary, I discussed, analysed, listened and learned hungrily with everyone and about anything that I thought could benefit my plan. This painstaking approach consumed me and contributed significantly to my ability to win some of the fierce battles against Michael and Ferrari.

If I look at my racing career, I was not the best driver. It may have been a physical or mental limitation that didn't allow me to deliver at the same level as Schumacher. However, by constantly striving to unleash my personal potential, when I was on form I was able to beat Michael and beat him well. I did absolutely *everything* I could possibly do to make the very best version of myself as a racing driver. On many occasions, that worked and I crossed the finish line first.

If you are serious about being the very best version of yourself, then the same demanding, time-consuming and exhaustive approach should apply to you. Does it?

CHAPTER 3
RISK

I don't see myself as a gambler. For example, I could never have been a motorbike racer. In my mind, those guys are taking far greater risks than I ever did in a Formula 1 car, even though certain elements such as my cornering speed was greater. However, I'm risk-averse. I'm not a daredevil. I was sent a YouTube video the other day of a girl leaning off the side of a building and she was letting this guy just hold her arm. I find that very frightening and had to watch through my fingers. That is a level of trust that is quite shocking, and for me personally the risk versus return was unacceptably high. Everyone's perception of risk differs.

I never felt at risk in Formula 1. You might find that a strange statement, but that's just how I felt. I didn't see it as an inherently dangerous occupation. For example, I never suffered a serious injury during my 15-year career. Some people would suggest that cornering a very complex F1 car at speeds of up to 180mph a few feet from a concrete barrier is one definition of risk, and I can understand that perception, yet my view on risk management sees that job very differently. I accept that as a Formula 1 driver I am fighting for two hours in a violent, physically demanding and, admittedly in the worst-case scenario, potentially life-threatening environment. However, I just didn't see that it was risky.

One of the fundamental aspects of Formula 1 is that we are not only trying to extract the maximum in performance but also manage risk. There is an old saying in racing: 'to finish first, first you must finish', so having reliable, robust technology is vitally important, and alongside that stands safety. Win or lose, we want to live to fight another day. We want to go home to our families at the end of the race.

Yet here is the single most stark example of how I was presented with a decision that was perceived by many to be a 'risk': my career in Formula 1 started because of one of the most serious accidents in the history of the sport, which caused the death of Ayrton Senna. Consequently, one of the questions that I get asked most frequently is, 'How does it feel to get your debut race drive after the man sitting in the car before you was killed?'

By 1994, my job as the test driver was to support our race drivers Damon Hill and Ayrton Senna by testing the car and helping with development. A three-times World Champion, Senna was already regarded as one of the sport's legendary stars. He certainly caused controversy on numerous well-documented occasions, but one element of Ayrton Senna that no one ever doubted was his commitment. An ace kart racer in the late 1970s, Senna turned to car racing in the early 1980s, and his commitment meant he didn't shy away from uprooting his life in Brazil and moving to the UK to drive in Formula Ford – with immediate success. By 1983 he was racing in Formula 3 for West Surrey Racing, winning the British Championship, before a direct move into Formula 1 with the tiny Toleman team in 1984. His passion and commitment were evident yet again when Senna astonished everyone by hauling the unfancied Toleman TG184 into contention, almost winning the rain-soaked Monaco Grand Prix. The race was controversially stopped early, with Senna catching race leader, 'local' hero and Frenchman Alain Prost. As a Lotus F1 driver he scored his maiden Formula 1 victory in a very wet Portuguese Grand Prix; this garnered him a reputation for being quick whatever the conditions and this was matched by an extraordinary skill at extracting additional performance during qualifying.

Senna became World Champion in 1988, as teammate to Prost at McLaren, when their historically dominant McLaren MP4/4 won 15 out of 16 races. However, the teammates' relationship was famously sour. Senna won titles again in 1990 and 1991 then joined Williams for 1994, aiming to benefit from the team's clear technical advantage the previous year, but a rule change that banned active, computer-controlled suspension systems came into force and detracted from the team's competitive edge. Nonetheless, you can imagine how remarkable it was for me to be around such a legend of the sport when I started working for Williams as a green-behind-the-ears test driver.

Unfortunately, at the 1994 San Marino Grand Prix, there were a series of very serious incidents starting on the Friday when my friend Rubens Barrichello was injured in a high-speed accident in his Jordan car. It would be preferable if I could stop my story there, but sadly this was not the end of it. It was a weekend that has gone down in history as a low point for Formula 1. On the Saturday, there was a really appalling accident when a young up-and-coming Austrian driver named Roland Ratzenberger was killed during qualifying. The following day, Ayrton was killed while leading the race when his Williams car speared off the track at the ultra-fast Tamburello curve, slamming into the barrier with Ayrton mortally wounded. Senna was pushing hard to maintain a lead over arch-rival Michael Schumacher at the time of his fatal accident. His state funeral in São Paulo, Brazil, illustrated the immense following that Senna had attracted, and his death created an iconic aura around one of Formula 1's most enigmatic personalities. There could have been no more blunt, tragic and high-profile reminder of the risk involved in Formula 1.

As the Williams test driver at the time, I was hugely affected by what I had seen. I wasn't actually at Imola on that day – I was at Silverstone. However, like everyone I expected to see him move, to get out of the car but, as with Roland, when you see them slumped in the cockpit, you fear the worst. Having two such tragedies compounded that shock. I have heard from people who were at Imola that there were a lot of tears, it was a terrible trauma. Many more tears were shed around the globe. Ayrton was so much more than a racing driver; in his home nation he was idolised as a national hero and that status applied all over the world. It was just the most massive shock.

The fatal accidents involving Senna and Ratzenberger had a huge effect on the sport of Formula 1. There had been fatalities before – Ayrton Senna was the 43rd Formula 1 driver to have been killed since the World Championship commenced in 1950 – but a number of things were very different this time. Unlike in the 1950s, '60s and '70s, these more recent incidents were fatal accidents broadcast live on television to hundreds of millions of fans around the world. It was on rolling news, 24 hours a day. It also happened to involve two drivers, on successive days, and one of those drivers was perhaps the greatest of his generation, arguably of all time. On top of the personal tragedy, my team, Williams, found itself at the centre of a court case with all of the stress, costs, damage to reputation and time that would take up. It was an incredibly sad and stressful time for everyone involved.

To be honest with you, I really didn't expect to receive a call from Frank Williams a few days later asking me to replace Ayrton Senna as the team's driver alongside Damon Hill. This was an immensely difficult time, we were all affected by what had happened to Ayrton. Yet here I was being given my big chance to race in Formula 1.

So, a few weeks after Ayrton's fatal accident I had to strap myself into the same specification of car, designed and built by the same team, run by the same mechanics, and go out and commit myself to driving flat-out. That meant I had to put aside any concerns about the equipment, the risk, the chances of me being hurt or worse, and go for it.

People often ask me, 'How on earth were you able to jump in that car and take such a risk?' I just didn't see it that way. I knew that the Williams team was doing everything to understand what had happened in that accident, and also to ensure that I had everything I needed in order to give me confidence in them and their car. This was a team that called itself Williams Grand Prix 'Engineering'. Engineering was at the heart of what they did, and I know that high-quality engineering and safety was a core value for them. This was a logical and very reassuring premise to take. I can genuinely say getting into that car did not trouble me; I knew this was a massive opportunity that had come my way, totally unexpectedly, but here it was. My ambition as a racing driver was to always drive the best cars and Williams was offering me exactly that.

I'm not going to pretend that I didn't contemplate the risk of getting in that car. However, I firmly believe that you mustn't let fear stop you making decisions. In Grand Prix racing there is a worst-case scenario and that is that you lose your life. Your car breaking down is bad, crashing off and retiring is also bad, but ultimately and tragically in the case of so many drivers over the years, the worst way your race can end is fatally.

Instead I saw it differently, in very black-and-white terms: my job was to take that Williams F1 car and race at speeds of over 200mph, totally trusting in my engineers and mechanics to have prepared it to be completely safe, reliable and high performing. My life, quite literally, was in their hands. Driving cars is what I knew, and I trusted in my team. I was comfortable with what I was being asked to do. You'd think given how I got my first seat, after a man was killed in a tragic accident, that I would be very sensitive to the risk in Formula 1, but it was just not how I saw it, not in the aftermath of Senna's death and not at any point in my 246-race career. I never felt I would die when I went out on track; crash, maybe, that is just being realistic, but die or suffer a life-threatening injury? No. I never, ever felt like that. Of course, I rationally understood the danger, but I'm not inherently a risk-taker, I never have been, and it just didn't seem risky in that way… I actually don't think I've ever done something that was risky.

Risk is all about perception. If a situation doesn't bother you, if there are no nerves, then that's great. Don't listen to people telling you that it is a dangerous situation, or a stressful presentation environment or whatever. For years, people told me that my job was very dangerous but I just never saw it that way. I am aware that some fans like to see a crash, it's just a part of some people's nature – an uneventful race with no on-track incidents is perceived as less interesting than one with people crashing off. Kids love the accidents, it's all very dramatic, and, to be fair, so do adults. I think it goes back to Roman times when thousands would turn up to watch gladiators quite literally fight to the death.

Closely allied with the analysis of risk is the ability to make decisions. If you can't make decisions in sport, business and life, you will struggle. The worst thing you can do is not make a decision. Armed with the information that is available to me at that time, I like to think I can make what will hopefully prove to be a logical decision. The only bad decision at any given time is no decision.

Why? Because, for example, if you don't make a decision in a racing car you'll crash. That might be a life-changing scenario, or worse. If you're prevaricating about a business decision, then hopefully it won't be life-threatening or risking some serious injury if you get it wrong, so just make the decision. I find indecision very off-putting. I would be very nervous about working with someone who couldn't make day-to-day decisions. Sport gives its protagonists a competitive advantage because we make decisions. Not always the right ones, maybe we choose the wrong tyres, or worse still the wrong braking point which leads to a crash sometimes. You made a decision, maybe it didn't work out but what we don't do in sport is sit on the fence.

So you gather all the information available to you and sit back, analyse then make the decision. One fascinating lesson that I picked up from Ron Dennis was about waiting till you have the best information available to you. He used to say, 'Why decide today if you don't have to, DC? Make sure you have all the very latest and most useful information before you decide.' The point where you absolutely have to decide is when you are armed with the best information available to enable you to make the right choice. Ron's approach isn't out of reluctance or indecision – it is a deliberate strategy to collate every single piece of relevant information that might be useful in as much depth as physically possible and then, and only then, make the decision based on those facts. If you are making a balanced, informed decision with all the information available then you are by definition reducing the risk.

One less tangible element of managing risk is to trust your instinct. Never underestimate the value of instinct in sport and in business. We are all born with an instinct to survive, but that can be honed and refined through experience and by being around successful people. Sometimes you just need to trust your gut instinct. If you have already achieved a degree of success in business, then you could argue that your instincts have served you well. That will have been aligned to hard work and application, of course, but we've all made decisions based on an instinct. This is a good thing.

This was what I did after Senna had been killed in terms of not chasing Frank for the drive. Everyone knew that one of the Williams cars was now empty. Some people were advising me to call up Frank and state my case for why I should get the drive. That didn't feel like the right thing to do, my instinct was telling me not to make that call. I'm not a salesperson, and I recognise that it is crucial to know when to stop selling. When Senna was killed, I didn't phone Frank up and ask after the seat that had now, through very tragic circumstances, become available. Certain drivers would have done that, but that's not how I work. I felt that my commitment in testing for the team, my attitude and application as well as my rapport with his engineers, would hopefully persuade him by example that I was the man for the job. These were horrible events that really shocked the whole world of sport, so there was also the feeling that a hasty sales pitch was just deeply inappropriate.

I ended up becoming a race driver in Formula 1 a year earlier than I expected. There was obviously the sense that this was a massive potential opportunity but I just felt in the circumstances that not selling myself to Frank was the right thing to do, because it was an emotionally charged moment. Williams F1 was experiencing a hugely demanding and stressful time and for me to push and hassle for a drive would not have been helpful or, in my opinion, in the best interests of the team.

Also, in emotionally charged moments, I think people like to make decisions that feel familiar. In extreme circumstances, people naturally don't want to take a decision which is high risk and unknown. That is what eventually transpired: Williams felt they knew me and my potential and so offered me the drive. During the season that followed, I ended up sharing that drive with Nigel Mansell who came in for a number of races but ultimately, Williams chose to go with me for the 1995 season. Waiting for Frank rather than harassing him after Senna's death turned out to be the right thing to do. That was my gut feeling, my instinct at the time.

I also had absolutely no intention of trying to negotiate more money – to be honest, the opportunity to jump in such an amazing team's car was something I'd have done for free. That first season in Formula 1 is also a good example of how certain risks need to be looked at from the viewpoint of opportunity rather than financial gain. Before the San Marino tragedies, I was earning £30,000 as a test driver for Williams, then after Senna was killed I did eight races and Frank Williams paid me £5,000 a race. So I earned £70,000 including finishing second in the Portuguese Grand Prix. Funnily enough, at the Canadian Grand Prix, I had to pay a withholding tax of £7,000 so it cost me £2,000 to come fifth! (At the same time, Damon Hill was earning around £500,000 a season.) When Nigel Mansell came in and did six races it was rumoured he was being paid a million per race. You might say, why would you accept a deal like that when the marketplace was paying so much more to certain drivers? That's irrelevant, or was to me at that time – that's what Frank offered and I went, 'Thank you very much Mr Williams' and got in the car. He gave me a massive opportunity and I knew that might lead to bigger and better things. It was a risk worth taking.

The next year I was paid half a million and the year after that I was earning several million. If I'd have argued over the initial £5,000 race fee on offer, Frank might have signed someone else and where would that have left me? Make sure you don't price yourself out of the market; understand that some jobs will pay better than others but some work will ultimately create huge opportunities that mean you will earn more in the future. It might feel like a risk if the money is modest but is it in fact a massive opportunity?

While we are mentioning Nigel Mansell, his story is full of moments when he took risks. I've touched on his absolute 'foot-to-the-floor' commitment in the car during an era when injury and death were commonplace, but there are also prime examples of his attitude to risk behind the scenes. Back in the days before Nigel had secured his first Formula 1 drive and he was still an emerging racer working hard to break through, there is one example of an enormous risk he took. For the 1978 season he needed to raise finance to continue his drive that year, so he sold his house and moved into rented accommodation; that was despite having saved and worked hard to buy that house for many years with his wife. Had the following season gone to plan, that risk-taking and faith in his ability would have been immediately rewarded; however, after just a handful of races, when those funds he had raised ran out, the team he was driving for terminated the relationship. Mansell was left with no drive, no money and no home. In fact, it would be another three difficult seasons before he finally got his break with Lotus, but that specific example shows you how certain people view risk differently to others.

Stepping away from the race track for a moment, I once did a talk for Tata Communications at a conference for business leaders, which was also attended by the musician and entrepreneur will.i.am. He was talking about taking risks and said, 'I came from the [LA housing] projects, from a house full of love but absolutely no money.' He grew up with the clothes on his back, a hot meal that his mum somehow managed to cobble together, and lots of love. 'The worst that can happen to me,' he explained, 'is that I go back to that, I go back to that happy place because I was a happy child. I've been there and it wasn't that scary.' So, essentially what he was saying is that all of his wealth, all of the adulation, all of the success can go, it just doesn't make him fearful. He is an international record producer, musician, businessman and multimillionaire, but he said nothing scares him about making business decisions because of that simple fact. That is a very profound and simple truth. That statement really resonated with me. The fear inside should not be allowed to create indecision. How bad can it be? Is it really that bad a risk?

One example of me taking a risk requires me to skip ahead in my story a little. After I retired from racing, I was signed up as commentator for the BBC's coverage of Formula 1. I had never done this before. Sure, I'd been interviewed thousands of times but that isn't the same. When you are being asked the questions like that, it is a very reactive experience, the presenter puts the questions to you and you respond in as much or as little detail as you see fit. I was used to that process and didn't find it nerve-racking at all. However, being a presenter is much more proactive, you are expected to fill the air time with credible, interesting content, you also have to fit into very specific time parameters, so you can't just waffle on for ages, there are very tight limits to what you can say. Plus, you are aware that if you mess up, you do so in front of hundreds of millions of people.

I remember going live for the first time in Melbourne for the Australian Grand Prix with Jake Humphrey and Eddie Jordan. We had earlier been through the proposed content and the timings with the director, to prepare us, but there is nothing quite like knowing you are now going live to millions of people. So I did find that experience more challenging than I had expected. Fortunately, I was with Jake who is a consummate professional, and he was able to guide and direct brilliantly. He is so adept as a host, he doesn't hog the air time, he always allows each of the speakers to voice their opinions. Quite quickly, as the season progressed I felt that Jake, Eddie and I had developed a good working relationship: we all knew when to chip in and when to sit back. Jake was the experienced presenter, I was the former racing driver and Eddie had been there, done that in terms of running a team. But yes, that very first day commentating and presenting was a lot more nerve-racking to me than people might think. In fact, I think it's fair to say it was actually far more nerve-racking than sitting in a racing car on the grid of a Grand Prix!

How you perceive and then manage risk will be crucial to your success. Like I said, I'm not a risk-taker. Some people are predisposed to jump, and others are more likely to think, *I don't fancy that*. I'll take the long way around. I am no gambler so I won't be parkour world champion any time soon. However, when an opportunity presents itself, I know how to assess that risk and I am never shy of making a decision. The combination of gut instinct allied with collating all the right information enables you to make a good decision and therefore challenge yourself. If I don't try a business idea that intrigues or challenges me, how will I know if I would've succeeded?

I've never had success at something that I didn't try.

CHAPTER 4
HOW TO BUILD A WINNING TEAM

Naturally, people often ask me about what it is like to drive a Formula 1 car. There is no doubt that it is a fantastic experience to drive something as light and powerful as a Williams, McLaren or Red Bull around the streets of Monte Carlo or on iconic circuits such as Silverstone and Monza. However, it is not the solitary experience that everyone imagines, because every step of the way I am supported by a group of people who are much cleverer than I am. I am merely one link in the chain that leads to success, and it all requires a team effort from start to finish, every day of the year, every minute of every day. Whenever you see a Formula 1 driver standing on the top step of the podium celebrating yet another Grand Prix victory, do not think for one moment that this is a purely individual achievement.

Growing up in a family which ran its own business, I think I gained an insight into the fact that success comes from a lot of hard work combined with people, and how they work together. Then, when I started racing as a young boy, initially in karting and then progressing into the different categories of racing that lead up to Formula 1, I always had very precise targets, and right from the very beginning I knew that I needed the best team of people around me to help achieve my goals. At the beginning, it was my family helping me, and later when I started racing with professional racing teams I realised that it was my engineers, mechanics and the team management who would give me the tools and support necessary to go out and win.

You hear the word 'team' bandied around Formula 1 all the time, and the fair-minded and down-to-earth drivers are the very first to thank their team when they win. I am proud to say that F1 really is one of the most exacting and outstanding examples of how teams can work to achieve great success. In order to illustrate this and therefore the concept of building a winning team, let me first detail what exactly a Formula 1 team consists of.

Let's start on race day itself. There is a core team of around 60 technical staff who travel to the races, servicing and rebuilding the car. They engineer it to suit the characteristics of each particular race track and work with me and my teammate to make sure that we have the best chance of winning on Sunday. Once I am out on track, my connection to the team is a two-way radio link with my race engineer who works directly with me on a day-to-day basis to help correlate all the information available to us and help me to optimise the performance of the car in the actual race. I am not an engineer, so while I don't understand all of the details of the car's aerodynamics, its vehicle dynamics, control systems, engine, gearbox and tyres, as the actual person racing the car I do know what I want from the car to enable me to give a race-winning performance against the competition.

The race engineer has to take my feedback and set about translating that into helping the engineering team understand where we have weaknesses and the need to improve. My race engineer will be supported by a small group of engineers and technicians at the trackside who are specialists in all of the systems within the car.

This is doubled up for all teams – each Formula 1 team has two cars so I will have a teammate who also has a race engineer along with his own support team, so we are already looking at a couple of dozen engineers and technicians responsible for helping me and my teammate extract the best performance possible. In an ideal world, all the information is shared between us, so that even my teammate, who I am ultimately racing against, is working alongside me in the meetings where we are trying to get the most out of the car each weekend.

We have a chief mechanic who oversees all the physical, mechanical changes to the cars and their specifications, to ensure that the correct adjustments are made, the right upgrades fitted and the overall set-up of the car is precisely as we want it. The chief mechanic will then have mechanics who have overall responsibility for different areas of each car, for example, the front suspension, the rear suspension, brakes and so on. So we have a clear hierarchy and responsibilities within the team, with everyone fully accountable for their area. In terms of the actual car on race day, if the wheel falls off, we know exactly who is responsible...

Aside from the engineers and mechanics who work directly with the drivers and on the cars, then we have logistics and operational staff to manage our freight and supply chain, as each team will bring two cars and around 30 metric tonnes of equipment to each race. Sometimes people want to know what the most important part of a Formula 1 car is; the answer is the part you don't have. So we need to have all the right parts, of the right specification, at the right time and in the right place on one of the 20 Formula 1 race tracks around the world. No excuses.

Aside from the technical staff, then there is the team management (including the team principal) who usually attends the races, looking after the business side of the sport; every team also has its commercial and marketing department, which handles customer relations with the sponsors, the hospitality, event management, public relations and so on. We are now talking about a small army of perhaps 90 to 100 people at every race, working flat out for five or six days to ensure that everything is in place to give us the best chance of success. Even our catering staff are vital because, as the saying goes, an army marches on its stomach and when we are racing in countries as diverse as Azerbaijan, Brazil, Singapore or Canada, having the correct diet, eating at the right times and keeping your energy level up is as vital for the mechanics as it is for me as a driver.

So, at each Formula 1 race we have 60 team members present to help us get the most out of the car, and give me the support necessary to go out and win the race. However, the remarkable thing is that this is only the tip of the iceberg because that race-day team represents only 15 per cent of our workforce, since 85 per cent of people who work for a Formula 1 team are based in a factory in the UK, Italy or Switzerland, designing, manufacturing, building and developing our product – the Formula 1 car – bringing it to the marketplace to sell to our customers – the sponsors – and providing all the back-office support from marketing to finance, HR to IT. A team of 800 to 900 full-time staff is pretty standard among the top teams in Formula 1, and they will then be supported by a supplier base of perhaps 200 companies providing everything from individual nuts and bolts to raw carbon composite materials, brake components and even engines.

This 'hidden' majority of the team work in all the functions you would find in any normal engineering business: research and development, design, manufacturing, quality testing, logistics, marketing, finance and administration. Yet they need them to have the same degree of motivation, focus and determination to succeed as the team members at the race track. The sheer number of people involved in this sport means that we absolutely have to get everyone aligned, working together and making sure they deliver. This complex, highly skilled, agile and multi-layered structure is why you hear people always saying that Formula 1 is a fantastic team sport. It is also why anyone looking in from the outside can learn so much from the sport in terms of teamwork. I have a very strong belief in the potential of a brilliant team and the ideas behind that. This is an inevitable consequence of working within Formula 1 for so long. Whatever career or role you find yourself in, you will need to know the importance of working in, or at least with, a team. Fortunately, I have been involved in one of the biggest F1 successes of the modern era, Red Bull Racing, which serves as a brilliant example of 'the power of teamwork'.

• • •

After I left McLaren in 2004, as I mentioned earlier there was a difficult period when I thought I would not be offered a drive by any team. As you know, Renault, Ferrari and Williams had all declined to work with me but I kept looking, kept persevering. I had also been talking to Jaguar – formerly Stewart Grand Prix prior to being bought out by Ford – and even met with them in Monaco during that year, but I really wasn't comfortable with certain members of the senior management. Overall, I also just didn't believe that Ford Motor Company and Jaguar were going to really make a difference – to be fair, I don't think they really believed in me either, so it went no further at that point.

Then Red Bull bought the team at the end of the year. At that point my contracts manager, ex-F1 driver Martin Brundle, was able to open up a conversation with the head of Red Bull Racing, Helmut Marko, that led very quickly to us agreeing a package. All it took was a change of ownership and a couple of alterations in senior management and suddenly I had total belief. Red Bull represented a fresh opportunity for me. I took some time to research and understand a little about this company that was relatively new to F1, to get my head around the motivations of its leadership team. The more I looked, the more I realised they were ambitious, hungry to succeed, and extremely focused on finding ways to beat the competition. Their brand was young, edgy and, of course, all about energy.

Taking the drive for Red Bull essentially secured me a huge pay cut and also a potentially significant drop down the grid from what I had been used to at McLaren. In fact, the wage I would be getting wasn't enough to cover my 'burn rate', my cost of living, because my life had expanded to include such things as planes and boats and all sorts. However, I believed I could make a difference to the team, that something very special could be created and, to be fair, we negotiated a bonus payment agreement for points scored and podiums secured. Nonetheless, it was still a massive drop in my guaranteed income. However, it was never about the money. I'm not motivated by money, although of course that is a nice by-product of working hard. Right from the very start of my career, the money was a nice perk of the job but the priority was racing. Ron Dennis always said that 'money is only important if you haven't got any…' I was lucky that this wasn't me. In situations like that, I think you really need to believe in your talent and the opportunity in front of you to make a difference, and so follow that belief as a priority over the money.

What I saw in Red Bull was *massive potential*. I'm happy and very proud to say that my instinct and analysis of the potential was correct: one of my most rewarding experiences was to use the final years of my racing career to help develop Red Bull Racing into becoming a dominant team, and when I scored their first podium finish in 2006 at the Monaco Grand Prix, we started an upward trend that ultimately led to the team and Sebastian Vettel winning four Constructors' and Drivers' World Championships. Sebastian became the youngest Grand Prix winner and the youngest World Champion because of the combined efforts of the team behind him; the designers, the manufacturing staff, the development team, their key technical partners and ultimately the mechanics who build and maintain the cars during a Grand Prix weekend.

None of this was a given when I joined. In fact, on the surface the opposite was probably more likely. Back in 1997 Jackie Stewart had returned to Formula 1 as a team owner, founding and leading Stewart Grand Prix alongside son Paul. The team was part-funded by Ford, and won the European Grand Prix at the Nürburgring,

Germany, in 1999, before Ford purchased the entire team in 2000 and rebranded it as Jaguar Racing. That set-up struggled and was eventually sold on, leading to the birth of Red Bull Racing. When Red Bull took over Jaguar, the team was not exactly top of the podium, so the achievement of taking a struggling F1 team and turning it into an operation that won four world titles provides us with an ideal example of how to build a winning team.

Many people in our sport were unconvinced that Red Bull could beat companies like Ferrari, Toyota and Honda in Formula 1. And yet that is exactly what they did. Perhaps inevitably, everyone wants to know how a company that revolves around an energy drink can produce a better Formula 1 car than a team like Ferrari or McLaren. The answer is in the culture of the company and its leadership; how they set high targets and have strategies to achieve those goals; how they empower and value all the staff; how they fill the company with the very best people; how they engender total commitment from the team by getting everyone to buy into the vision, the way they innovate and their ability and willingness to respond very quickly to challenges and opportunities. In Formula 1 everyone likes to talk about the technology, the complexity and the finance involved, but in reality all the top teams have great technology, big factories and good budgets, so the characteristic that differentiates performance is the team culture. That's how Red Bull Racing set themselves apart from all their competitors.

Firstly, let's start at the very top, with the Austrian businessman Dietrich Mateschitz who founded the Red Bull energy drinks business in 1984. Having previously worked for companies including Unilever and Blendax, as part of a business trip to Thailand Mateschitz tried a caffeinated tonic drink there. Recognising that European consumers loved caffeinated tea and coffee, yet had no soft drink alternative, he launched Red Bull in Austria in 1987 as a means of exploiting that gap in the market. In doing so, he effectively created the energy drinks sector, and to this day Red Bull remains the dominant brand around the globe.

A marketeer by profession, Mateschitz took a non-traditional approach to promoting Red Bull from the outset, eschewing advertising in favour of using events and guerrilla marketing tactics in order to enable consumers to sample the product directly. His triple passions for motor racing, winter sports and aviation were used to create compelling sponsorships and marketing activities, with Red Bull's highly successful motorsport's activities running in parallel to extreme sports and events such as the world famous Red Bull Air Race. His remarkable collection of aircraft, all of which can still fly and date back to the earliest days of aviation, is housed in Mateschitz's extraordinary Hangar 7 facility at Salzburg airport.

Mateschitz's path to owning an F1 team is inspiring. He had been involved in Formula 1 sponsorships throughout the 1990s, but he tired of not getting the results he demanded. He had already spent 20 years building Red Bull into a successful company and he now wanted to combine the success of the brand with the global marketing power of Formula 1. So that is why he purchased the stumbling Jaguar Racing team from Ford Motor Company for a nominal sum in 2004. He later sanctioned the purchase of the Minardi Formula 1 team in September 2005, rebranding it as Scuderia Toro Rosso, effectively using it as a junior team to develop such talents as Sebastian Vettel, Daniel Ricciardo, Max Verstappen and Carlos Sainz Jr. He delegates the overall management of the motorsport programme to former Austrian F1 driver Dr Helmut Marko. A unique and compelling character, Dietrich Mateschitz is a highly results-driven individual and demands the same from all his businesses, not just the motor-racing activities.

When I first met Dietrich Mateschitz, I realised how passionate he was about Formula 1 and putting his brand at the forefront of our sport. He represents a fine example of how any successful team needs a great leader. He is a very impressive individual and I have learnt a lot from him about how to do business. His is a very imposing personality, but he is also incredibly empowering of the people around him. In terms of his approach to Red Bull Racing, he often turns up at the Grands Prix but maintains a low profile. He's not one for questioning every person, what are they doing, why are they doing it. Of course, he will, I'm sure, give them the value of his opinion at the right moment but the rest of the time he empowers them to run the ship. Ultimately, he employs over 800 people just within the Red Bull Racing team, plus a huge workforce around the world for the rest of his empire, so of course he can't know everyone's name. However, he lets the people he employs get on with their job and expects them to do it to the best of their ability. He is able to do this because he trusts that the management he has put in place will employ the right people and then individual managers of the departments will in turn employ the right people to have the best representation of Red Bull on the race track.

One of those key individuals is Christian Horner, Red Bull Racing team principal since 2005. Christian started his career inside the cockpit before deciding to hang up his racing helmet at the end of 1998. Prior to that he had raced with moderate success in Formula Renault, Formula 3 and Formula 3000, but at the relatively young age of 25 he decided that his talent for business outweighed his skills behind the wheel. He established Arden Motorsport as a highly successful team in Formula 3000, the feeder category to Formula 1 at that time, winning the team's championship for the final three years of its existence, 2002–2004 inclusive. The 2004 title was won by Horner's lead driver Vitantonio Liuzzi, who enjoyed the financial backing of Red Bull, and this success was pivotal in Christian being asked by Dietrich Mateschitz to become his new team principal at Red Bull.

Great champions and top business people lead from the front, they are generals taking the soldiers into battle. They are not superhuman, but they have power and belief in their convictions, and they know how to get all their team aligned and fighting for the same cause. The great leaders show that by being as committed to the cause as anyone else, if not more so. Sir Alex Ferguson has said the most important person in a football team is the manager because if you lose control of the team it all falls apart.

In terms of being a leader, whether that's a small local business, a Formula 1 team or a huge multi-national corporation, the challenge is ultimately the same: getting the best from a group of people. It is not easy, otherwise everyone would do it, but if you are very clear about your own personal targets and objectives, and you can inspire those around you to take their responsibilities very seriously and deliver for you, it's truly amazing what can be achieved together.

As leader, you set so much by example. Case in point: it is true that the atmosphere at Red Bull is more relaxed than other teams. This comes from the very top. Many people commented on how I seemed more relaxed once I joined that team, citing the fact I grew stubble as a sign that the regime was less strict. It was certainly less strict than the McLaren way, but don't be fooled that life at Red Bull was more loose or slack, it certainly wasn't. I can tell you that the heavy work ethic was exactly the same. A key difference was that when Christian walked through the factory, people felt they could engage with him and chat, whereas with someone like Ron, for example, people were not so inclined to do that. So, it's just different management styles, and let's be honest, both have worked.

Great leaders also know the difference between delegating and handing over completely – you need to empower individuals, but as a leader you also need to be the one that is aware of what is happening with the big picture. If you just look at your managers as people to take workload off your desk so that you can forget about it, then you will fail: a great leader will always actively mentor and coach his team. In my business life, not everything has worked out as well as it could have or should have, but when things haven't worked out, in many instances it has been because I haven't been able to be hands on. When you are hands on, you can guide and shape your business. It's not about just handing over and then switching off, it's having ownership, still having input because you care, and that's very important.

For the leadership of any team, it is vital that clear, precise and high targets are set. Again, Red Bull were laser-focused in this area. Dietrich Mateschitz is a great example of someone who sets high goals. He has done so much more than start a drinks business from scratch; as I pointed out earlier, he effectively created the energy drinks industry – an entirely new breed of soft drink. When it came to entering Formula 1, from the moment Red Bull Racing was established, he saw his team as a challenger, threatening the establishment, and innovating in areas where other teams were afraid to experiment. He was never going to shy away from the competition and set mediocre goals. In business and sport, there needs to be total clarity of ambition. If you can't understand or articulate your goal, then you are going to be beaten before you even start. Mateschitz is a classic example of a businessman knowing precisely what his goals were. In the winter of 2004, I'd met with Dietrich before signing the contract to drive for Red Bull. He told me he wanted it to be a winning team. He told me that his goal was to make the team respected in the paddock as competitors and then to build it to be capable of winning a world title both with a driver and as a constructor. In return I told him that his goal was going to take a serious amount of investment and all the rest of it. He said, 'Yes, I understand, that's why you guys are here. Tell me what we need, this is my ambition, let's make this a winning team.' Now, that's a pretty straightforward statement. That's the brief. Uncomplicated. So that's what we did. It didn't happen by accident, it happened by planning, commitment, empowerment and the people within the team. However, without the clarity of vision on day one from the very top, that could not have happened.

Ambitious goals and targets are all very well but you need a team strategy to achieve them. One aspect of F1 that I endeavour to apply to my business interests is having a precise strategy, something I touched on earlier in terms of its relevance to personal potential. Formula 1 is hugely driven and focused around strategy during the race. We all see how F1 teams have a tyre strategy in a race and that can be the difference between victory and perhaps not even being on the podium. The race strategy deployed by Formula 1 teams is largely analogous to business strategy in that each team has to look at all of the variables likely to affect its performance and determine how to manage those better than the competition.

Let me take you on a quick detour into F1 race strategy as an example of the detail and thought you need to put in to a winning strategy for your team. A winning F1 race strategy requires a number of key elements. There are a host of variables to consider from an operational standpoint, including making sure the car is legal and compliant with the rules, since there is no point trying to win with a product that will be disqualified. Then there is product safety and quality, ensuring that it will be safe for the driver and team to operate, and have the necessary inherent quality needed to finish the race.

Strategy will vary race to race, just as business strategy sometimes needs to flex market to market, so what works in Australia might not work in Japan, or what delivers a victory in Monaco might be a fiasco at Silverstone. It is vital that everyone in the team is aligned behind the specific strategy and that there are not going to be time-wasting arguments mid-race. Everyone has to know what the strategy is, and their part in delivering that.

This is where execution comes into place, since in order for the strategy to be delivered the team has to execute every aspect to perfection. No excuses. This includes the drivers in obeying team instructions, using their tyres, brakes, engine and gearbox in the right way throughout, and pitting on the correct lap to deliver the pit-stop strategy. Or it could be the pit crew in making certain that they know which driver will pit on which lap, ensuring that they are ready to deliver a two-second service and, of course, to have the type and compound of tyres at the ready.

The other aspect of strategy is being prepared to change direction if necessary, whether due to external factors such as weather or an incident involving competitors, or even because the competition does something unexpected. Having the agility, and ability, to rapidly adjust strategy is important, because it makes no sense to plough on regardless when it is clear the race is developing in an unexpected way. We are not interested in a post-mortem about why it all went wrong when it was plainly obvious that changes to strategy needed to be made in real-time.

This is how strategy plays out in F1 and, as I said, not all of it is necessarily applicable to business. However, there are many parallels that I take with me into my business life. I always try to have a strategy in my mind, even if I don't necessarily write it down in a meticulous business plan. I spend private moments just going through in my mind, conversations with myself if you like, *What is the best strategy for this project?* By 'strategy' I mean a set of tactics and processes backed up by a precise allocation of resources, with the specific objective of achieving a particular goal. If you are in a senior role, a decision-making position, you have to have formulated a strategy in your mind as you see it before you can then open it to the team.

Don't get overwhelmed by obsessing over business strategy. My general approach is very simple – one step at a time. Break the process down into smaller pieces and then focus in on each one of those steps. By definition, if you make every one of those steps the most efficient it can be, then your journey as a whole will be much more productive than a team who has a lesser strategy. Then apply the same process for the next mile, and the next and so on. It sounds simple, and of course it might not be in terms of the detail, but in essence this approach is easy to conceptualise and execute.

This is where Red Bull and Mateschitz aced their challenge. Once he had set his clear and high goals and had a strategy in place to accomplish that, Mateschitz committed to that goal with resources and focus. F1 is not the cheapest sport, that's no secret, so to achieve those goals he had to invest a very significant sum of money. However, this wasn't money just thrown in haste at a vanity project. This was a very carefully considered investment. Any investment is looking for a return. Red Bull invested that money because they believed that the marketing return on that investment would ultimately increase the profile and desirability of the brand and they would sell more drinks. This was all part of Mateschitz's over-arching strategy. Of course, money will not buy you success, but what it gave Red Bull was the ability to put in place the right people, the structure, the tools and the facilities to create a winning team.

First up in that list is the people, the single most important element of any organisation. Crucially, Christian Horner headed up a young, motivated and empowered team. Dietrich motivated and invested in that team. In turn, that allowed other key people to be persuaded to come and join. The new Red Bull team also quickly removed the people who they felt were slowing the process down and although that is never an easy thing to do, that was a key part of the strategy to realise the team goal. Some people in management defend their position by stifling creativity. That might be because they want to hold on to all the keys, as I mentioned earlier, or because they feel threatened by more junior talent. They may fulfil a need for a given time, but ultimately if they are allowed to continue to stifle the energy and process of the team, they will have to go. If something is not quite right in your team, you have got to address it straight away. That is the problem with sweeping something under the carpet – the dirt is still there, it will just come to light at some later point. There have been people who I have worked with in Formula 1 that I didn't particularly warm to and felt that I could find someone better. It was never my decision to have them removed, but what I could do was present my case to the team principal as to why I thought this person was holding back the team or creating difficulties. I can't claim that I've had to have that conversation very often and it's certainly not something I relish. That's always a tricky conversation to have because it involves people's career and finances. There is no such thing as 'not taking it personally' when things like that happen in business. How can you not take that personally? However, sometimes it has to be done, I don't enjoy it and I don't like it but it is sometimes necessary to move the team forward. Some people might regard that as ruthless. What I will say is that you have to have conviction. You've got to know what it is you are trying to achieve. You have to be intolerant of average. If you are to maintain your team's focus and productivity, then any negativity in a relationship is unhelpful at best, debilitating at worst.

Of course, if you remove people from the team then there are roles that need to be filled. This is the next area of team-building where Red Bull excelled – their ability to recruit the very best people to their project. Part of my involvement in the team was to help them achieve this. The objective was to give the team a better chance of achieving success by having the very best people available, sharing in their knowledge, spreading the right mentality, skills and personal ambition on the journey towards success. All the great F1 teams are filled with positive, energised and very driven individuals. Surrounding yourself with people who share a winning mentality is incredibly powerful. You have to recruit people who want to work together in the same high-pressure environment to build a successful outcome.

Red Bull approach this in two ways: firstly, for certain key roles, they attract the very best talent that already exists in the field.

For example, I helped them to target the recruitment of technical director Adrian Newey, who I had worked with at both Williams and McLaren, as I knew he would provide strong technical leadership and direction, plus obviously brilliant designs. Adrian had actually considered a move to Jaguar Racing back in 2001 but when I started working for Red Bull and the subject of who was the premier designer to employ came up, it was very clear that Adrian was the man that the team needed. This was the kind of key appointment that helped us turn around the team's fortunes, because Adrian knew how to get the best out of a group of engineers and also happened to be one of the greatest engineering brains of his generation. In his book, *How to Build a Car*, Adrian recalls how he phoned me after being offered the Red Bull job and did what he called a 'sanity check', by which he means he wanted my opinion on whether Red Bull really were what they were claiming to be. I remember the call, I replied, 'Adrian, this is the real deal, these guys are absolutely committed to making this a successful team.' I believe on that basis he agreed to come on board. That was a big jump, leaving a team as historically successful as McLaren to go to a new set-up with no previous collective experience in F1. So he sanity checked with someone he trusted. I'm very flattered that the person was me.

Headhunting top talent isn't a technique exclusive to Red Bull, of course. Many F1 team owners and bosses throughout history such as Lotus's Colin Chapman, Sir Frank Williams and

McLaren's Ron Dennis are highly competitive individuals with a very clear and focused strategy on winning and they do that by bringing together the very best people, and the best partners, to build a winning package and to focus on what is important. You don't need to be an F1 team owner to do this – whatever your business or role, surround yourself with the very best.

The second way that Red Bull energised their recruitment process was by tapping into the youth market. Just as their drinks are bought in massive quantities by the younger market, then so too did the recruitment staff at Red Bull, under the guidance of the team leadership, source the very best young and undiscovered talent. Red Bull has to be about pushing the boundaries and bringing on the youth market and young talent. A lot of the brand values of Red Bull are viewed with great envy by rival companies, that sense of edginess and energy. Youth is where new opportunity lies. So Red Bull Racing gave talented young people an opportunity. That was reciprocated by the loyalty and energy these new faces poured into the company, but they also brought along fresh ideas. It was a win–win.

As an aside, sometimes you can get unexpected people joining in on your team, and not always for the best reason. Back in 1995 during the British Grand Prix at Silverstone, I was racing very hard and, as always, wanting to give the British fans a great race. Suddenly my race radio crackled into life.

'Dave, Dave…'

'Yes?' I asked, rather puzzled by them not using 'DC'. *I wonder which member of my team this is and what the team order will be?*

'All right, Dave, er, can you do a 2.30 pick-up in Towcester?' It turned out a local taxi firm's radio had picked up my car radio frequency and they were calling a driver who just happened to be called David. Obviously, the taxi request was pretty urgent so I just politely said, 'Sorry, I can't, I'm a wee bit busy right now…'

• • •

Once you have your leaders in place who specify a goal and a strategy, and your team of talent is recruited, next up you need to be very familiar with the actual personnel in order to field your best race-day line-up. Part of that awareness of your staff is knowing who is correct for which role. If you have a super-friendly, likeable guy with good knowledge, then putting him in the backroom with no customer-facing role is pretty pointless; equally, if you have a super-geek who knows more about certain aspects of the business than anyone but is socially awkward and quite cold, then don't put him on the front desk. It's unfair on both to expect them to excel in environments they are not at their best in. You also need to review these roles because people change. I'm 47 as I write this, and a different person from the one I was when I was racing in my twenties and thirties. So if your staff are with you for a long time, keep reviewing their strengths and weaknesses.

Many people look at their team and pick up on the limitations of their peers and colleagues. However, to truly succeed in a team you need to be acutely aware of your *own* limitations. I'm absolutely comfortable with understanding my limitations and therefore I don't have any hang-up with that. Of course, I would love to be academically brighter and multilingual, for example, but that hasn't come naturally to me. If I really wanted to change any of those things I would have to commit time to improving them, but that would mean I wouldn't be giving time to the things that I am more naturally adept at. So I like to be aware of my limitations, focus on the elements I can help to create and recognise that other colleagues have different skill sets that I don't that will benefit the team. Perhaps there's an element of looking at your own ego here: are you really saying you are the most talented, multi-skilled person in the team? Do you really have no areas where others could offer benefits and skills? Don't be that arrogant. Apply these obvious rules to your business. This can only come from knowing yourself and your team really well, their strengths and weaknesses, best attributes, worst flaws, then figure out how to shape your team using that information.

The next key element of Red Bull's success after getting the right people in the right jobs was that once they were recruited, the leadership team *let them do their job*. People were given the freedom to take ownership, make their own decisions, and act much more quickly than before. Until we get to the point where artificial intelligence shapes decisions, it's always going to be down to individuals and if you get a group of motivated and empowered individuals coming together and working together, the potency can be incredible.

This means making sure that every single person in the company understands how critical their role is, and feels part of the journey that the business is on. Red Bull encourages discussion and feedback, rather than simply dictating how they want things to be done. Time and again they find that the people at the sharp end of any job – or role – can give great ideas and insights into how they can do their work better. Part of that process is to make sure that everyone involved understands their strengths and weaknesses. Sometimes we find that someone else in the room will come up with a better solution, a more efficient outcome to a problem, but because we are lined up and focused on the same goal, we have the strength to be flexible and accommodate that.

This drives a culture where every job is regarded as critical and each person is fully accountable. As a team at the cutting edge of F1, Red Bull cannot afford to have anyone ignore the role they play in making sure that the team achieve their targets. This is why one of the interesting aspects of teamwork is the fact that, while some people think it is about collective responsibility, in reality teamwork is all about each and every individual being the best they can be in whatever role or position they hold. This goes back to Chapter 2, unleashing your own personal potential. I have lost count of the number of times Formula 1 races have been lost because someone, somewhere, did not do their job properly. Considering the high stakes, it is not surprising how much effort is put into making sure that everyone is made accountable and asked to take full responsibility for the job they do.

This might all sound very idealistic, this utopian team where everyone gets on, takes personal responsibility and has a wonderful time winning world titles every year. Of course not, no team is free of tension, disagreements and personality clashes. However, you don't necessarily need to surround yourself with like-minded people to create the best team, because I think as long as everyone is aligned on where you are aiming for, it can still work. You might not want to sit with a certain person for a ten-hour flight, but by showing them respect in the workplace, you are making them feel empowered and engaged and that can only be a good thing for everyone. Managing different egos and keeping the volatile parts separate for as long as necessary is a skill of managing a team, but so is recognising that we will need to bring those people together at certain points. With McLaren, Ron Dennis famously had to find a way to keep Alain Prost and Ayrton Senna working on the same team, so I hope your own challenges with personnel that don't get along will be somewhat less dramatic!

I'm not proposing that you expect to be life-long pals with everyone you work with, that clearly isn't going to happen. In fact, to be accepting of the variations of others is an absolutely key aspect of being able to work in teams and get the best out of people. You need to be able to think, *I don't really warm to this individual, but he or she has skills that I don't that are essential for me to be able to achieve what I would like to do.*

In those instances, it is important to be able to professionalise relationships and understand how they each work. Some people you absolutely build a bond with, you enjoy the friendship and that may last a lifetime; other people you work with will never be your friend and that is fine, you just need to recognise the difference. They are providing a role that you need to achieve your goal and likewise they may well need you to achieve their goal – that just completely decouples the need to actually like the individual. There needs to be a common 'need'. Mutual respect is not enough, there has to be that 'need' – that's what makes those types of business relationships work.

You can also have different modus operandi compared to people you are very fond of, and this need not get in the way of building a winning team either. Now, as you know from my days of polishing the underside of my karts, I like everything in order. Maybe not the 'every pencil straight on the desk' kind of order that my dad and people like Ron Dennis prefer, but I do like tidiness and neatness. However, my very good friend, the legendary designer Adrian Newey, is not the same as me in this way. Sometimes he opens his briefcase in front of you and it looks like a bomb has gone off in there. To an outsider that might look like chaos but the point is

Adrian knows exactly what is inside and where, in his brilliant mind he has everything to hand and he is totally comfortable with that. Adrian is… well, he's not quite a mad scientist but in that briefcase, as in design, he sees things that other people can't. That type of creative genius can be like that and, let's face it, his methods have worked for him so far! I could not work that way but I'm not Adrian, so you have to have scope for accommodating other people's approaches – as long as you are aligned it can work brilliantly. With Adrian, his record-breaking career success means that people know he delivers, so they don't care if his briefcase is tidy or not. Teamwork takes all shapes and sizes.

Another absolutely crucial element of building a winning team that Red Bull excel at is ensuring that you make everyone – and by that I mean *everyone* – feel *valued*. A common problem I see with high-level business people is a failure to respect everyone in their business – not just other executives or managers but right down to the receptionist worker or the cleaner. It's simple human courtesy but it also makes a lot of sense. Remember people's names, take an interest in their life; of course, if you run a business of 1,000 people you can't remember everyone, but there will be a circle of people that you come into regular contact with so don't ignore those who are not higher up the ladder than you.

It's not just politeness, there's a practical reason for this. If you don't value any one person in the chain, results will suffer. For example, what makes a great restaurant? Is it really the food on the plate? Having been left waiting for a table, or served by a miserable waiter, does that really get cancelled out by an amazing piece of meat? Even if the steak was that good (that's some steak), then the simple fact is if the waiter had been welcoming and the table ready on time, the whole experience would have been even better. People put so much attention on what are perceived as key roles – in this example a talented head chef – but fail to train, value and respect the waiter or maître d' who is the first point of contact, the first impression. You've got to make people feel valued and engaged.

Being a good leader isn't just about having a strategic plan for the business, it's often just spending time with your team, and by that I mean everyone in your team, not just the board or the senior managers, but all your staff. What you want is a cleaner who aspires to be a receptionist; a receptionist who aspires to be an office manager; an office manager who wants to be a regional manager; a regional manager who wants to be on the board, and so on. If you are starting with people who have no ambition it can be very difficult to move things forward. Spend time with the team, *real-time…* do you have people like that?

If you have lost perspective as a CEO or owner or senior manager of a company, then you may well ask why you need to engage with, and look after, the workers who are much lower down the staff structure. However, think about it like this: ensuring that the person on the front desk is engaged in the company is very important, because if they are not, what if they don't put a call through to you at five o'clock because they don't feel valued, instead they think, *I want to go home, my boss won't appreciate my extra diligence anyway, I'll let that go through to answerphone.* That might've been a call that changes the fortunes of the company but instead the contract ends up with a rival. I had an experience that illustrates this when I first became involved in co-owning a hotel called The Columbus in Monaco, around the time I was racing with McLaren. One of the things that made me interested in becoming involved in a hotel business was the fact that I have spent most of my life travelling, and therefore I believe I know what represents good or bad customer service. Anyway, on this particular day, I phoned up to make a booking and the person who answered just didn't really seem that engaged. So I walked out of my apartment, wandered round to the hotel reception and when I got there the staff were all like, 'Ah, Mr Coulthard, how are you?' – a very different attitude. So I explained to that person a few ways I thought they could do that differently. I chatted with them, engaged with them and spent time getting to know them, so that they felt a part of what the hotel was trying to achieve.

Do you introduce yourself to members of staff lower down the company order? Do you ask them their names? Do you know anything about them at all? I occasionally do so-called 'meet-and-greets' where fans come along to say hello, and they can be fun, although I'm not going to pretend the notion of people queueing to meet me isn't something I find slightly puzzling. Anyway, they do, and I always introduce myself, 'Hi, I'm David', which seems to cause some bemusement. I can see why, but it's a common courtesy. So if you are a high-level executive and you walk into a room with people who might not work with you on a daily basis, pay them the simple respect of introducing yourself. Likewise, in my opinion you should not be so time-poor that you don't even shake hands with employees or co-workers. That fleeting fraction of a second leaves a lasting bad impression, in my view. Never forget the importance of engaging with people. When you come into a room, no matter how 'important' you are perceived to be, does it really take that much effort to simply shake everyone's hand?

These are little things that make people feel special so why would you not do that when it takes no more time or effort, yet you can make people feel better about themselves and more engaged and willing to work and be positive about the business. That can only be a good thing, surely? This level of instinctive understanding only comes with time and with really getting to know people, you can't 'cheat' it. Christian Horner is very good at this, he is approachable and accessible and that is a popular and beneficial way to do things.

Of course, not everyone would agree with my method. Ron Dennis is known for running a very strict ship, and you can't deny that he has built up an amazing company that employs thousands of people over many years using his more regimented approach, so it's not a one-size-fits-all. This is just how I see it.

If an individual is fulfilling a role in your workplace, then in my opinion you have a responsibility as the CEO or owner to know about that person – because it is respectful, and that engagement will fuel their passion about the business, which in turn will make them a better worker and therefore drive better returns, so everyone wins. If your staff are not committed because you pay them no attention and show them no respect then, like any relationship, it will begin to fail.

There is a simple way to examine this topic at work: what would your team say about you if they could speak openly and honestly? If they would say you're an idiot, then clearly you are failing to lead your team. Don't be unapproachable and unlikeable at work. Sounds simple but, let's face it, we all know people like this, don't we? Sure, there are stories of business leaders who are notoriously difficult people, but we don't need to use them as justification for being the same. Perhaps ask yourself the question: *How many work colleagues will be at my funeral?* How many will be there because they were moved by you as an individual? How many will be there because they've got to go? If you are a difficult or unpopular boss, then how can you possibly expect to build a winning team?

Another question to ask in terms of negative elements within a team is what do you do if the ideal environment doesn't exist, if your team does not support you? As I mentioned earlier, it's no secret that during my time at McLaren, I felt that Ron clearly favoured my teammate Mika Häkkinen. This led to a quite crippling issue with my self-confidence and eventually became quite a toxic situation in terms of my performance. If you feel you are unsupported at work, then all you can do is present your concerns in a polite, measured and concise way, hope that the team appreciate your issues and are inclined to make changes to accommodate the problems. At the same time, you have to continue to be at your very best, do everything you can to unleash your personal potential. Do not waver just because everything isn't perfect.

The final aspect of Red Bull's team-building prowess that is worth mentioning before I move on to other examples is their operational agility. When I first drove for Red Bull Racing, part of my job was to provide feedback on where the team had been going wrong previously, when it was known as Jaguar Racing. I soon picked up on the fact that there were cultural elements that needed to change. The Jaguar Racing team had huge potential, yet it had not been a winning team. It had failed to produce a truly competitive car, and there was a tendency for people to come up with excuses as to why it was not winning. There was also a surprising lack of quality in its engineering, and this meant they were spending a lot of time focusing on reliability problems rather than performance. There were plenty of talented people, but many of them were spending time writing reports and analysing past failures. They were not sharing knowledge or being frank about the real issues they were facing. They were moving too slowly in an environment that demands speed, agility and fast decision-making. Without wishing to criticise the old Jaguar Racing team too much, they spent a lot of time using historic information to look at the past, while at Red Bull Racing the focus was on using data *to plan for the future*. As an F1 driver, I am mainly interested in what lies ahead; what's around the next corner or what we have coming from research and development that will help us to achieve a higher level of performance at the next race. Truly historic data is of little interest to me; of course I want to know what has happened in the last race, the previous qualifying or in the practice we have just completed. So, we spend a lot of time looking at that. But ultimately we are only doing that to learn and move forward. In my opinion, when the team was Jaguar it had just become bogged down with reporting and layers and layers of process because of the corporate requirements of Ford Motor Company. All these reports had to be sent to Detroit, there appeared to be this sort of corporate-suit mentality which was stunting progress and stifling the creativity and energy of the team. When Red Bull came in and bought the team, they just got rid of that philosophy and structure, and immediately focused less on reporting the past and more on creating the future.

So instead of writing long reports we asked people to look at the information that would give us the best clues as to where we were going wrong, how we could improve, and quickly implement the changes necessary. We encouraged feedback, and stimulated debate about the areas where we could do better. In Formula 1, you need to work quickly and make fast decisions. Red Bull knew this was important if they were going to beat the big car manufacturers. We were not as large, but we used our size to our advantage. So you can see that a key part of the quick success of Red Bull taking over from the Jaguar team was all about becoming less corporate and more 'business agile'.

When you are involved in a top team functioning at such a high level, it is incredibly rewarding. As one of Red Bull Racing's drivers, I watched the team develop their strikingly high-performance culture and it has been incredibly motivating to be part of a team that is pushing hard to succeed, every day, and being the best that they can be. Ultimately, they did what they set out to do: win both the Drivers' and Constructors' World Championships no less than four times, from 2010 to 2013 inclusive. That suggests they were doing something right; in fact, it is probably one of the best examples of team culture and ethos triumphing over competitors with greater resources and heritage in the industry.

. . .

Moving aside from Red Bull, there are many other brilliant examples in F1 that illustrate the crucial importance of creating a winning team. On a personal level, most of the great champions I have been around know how to get the very best out of their team. They know to respect the chain of command, empower everyone in the team, be aware of the strengths and weaknesses of each individual and work with people even if they don't particularly get along with them on a personal basis. Many of the great F1 drivers are mavericks, really strong, exaggerated personalities who perhaps, at least from the outside, might look like they are pretty selfish, consumed with their own brilliance and so on. In fact, I think that many people would be very surprised to find that actually many of the very top drivers are incredibly skilled at being team players and interacting with their team, mechanics, engineers. Yes, they want to win and they may have rivalry with other drivers, but behind the scenes you might be amazed at just how adept and talented these people are at working within a team.

Clearly, drivers such as Senna and Prost were not necessarily ever going to be the best of friends when they were teammates, but within the team they both knew how to maximise the people around them for the best performance. They were focused on delivery and part of that is understanding how to get the best out of all the team members, not just the team manager.

For example, at times in his career it is fair to say that Alain Prost was perceived by many as very political, a man who could cleverly manage people and events in the paddock and his garage to best suit his chosen goal, which was to win the world title. Some of his critics might say that dilutes his achievements on the track but in my opinion that isn't so. To keep all sides happy in an intense and hugely competitive world such as F1 is not easy. Prost was simply using his skills to make sure every tiny element of his day was working towards the goal of being champion.

Fernando Alonso is seen by some people as quite divisive. Mark Webber says he is a little bit like a grenade in a team, there will be some collateral damage. He left McLaren early, he left Ferrari early, and arguably he would have won more world championships than he has actually got if that hadn't been the case. Is that because he is a bit divisive or is that just because of fate? Lewis Hamilton has at times been seen as divisive, certainly he can be outspoken and offer strong opinions, but his results speak for themselves. Prost, as I mentioned, was seen as political and Senna was also a polarising figure. However, what you cannot deny about all of these people is their incredibly high level of success. They are all very good at subtly getting people behind them, getting people to believe in them, to work for them; all these guys are just very committed to the team, because they know that the team is the catalyst for their opportunity. Clearly, they may not have compatible personalities out of the cars but they view the importance of the team in the same way. As a viewer, you only see the two hours or so of the race on TV, but there are another 160+ hours in a week for these drivers to be at the factory, in the garage, testing, doing media work, sponsor relations, where their treatment of the team around them could negatively influence their chances of success at the race weekend. It's pretty relentless and these are men who have finely honed their approach to overcoming these challenges. So it's no coincidence that they are all world champions.

For my part, another aspect of a winning team is having a culture that respects the chain of command. Any team can crumble if people do not respect roles above them, as well as below. Let's fast-forward to my role as a TV presenter at the 2017 Mexico Grand Prix where I was working for Channel 4. Lewis was about to win the world title for the fourth time and one of the broadcast team asked for me to meet and interview him at the end of the race. In order to do that, I had to leave the commentary booth about ten minutes before the final lap. But they didn't want me to go that early, because it would mean Channel 4 would lose my commentary input on the final laps. The risk was there might be an incredible finish to the race and I would not be commentating on that. However, because the finish line was a good long way from the commentary booth, there was no way I could leave it too late otherwise I would miss my slot with Lewis. Plus, when I got there, I needed a few seconds spare to catch my breath and prepare for the fact that instead of broadcasting to three million people on Channel 4, I would suddenly be talking to several hundred million people around the world. The simple fact was that broadcasting to that huge global audience – all the broadcasters have to take that feed – was a great opportunity and not to be missed. So although I listened to this particular individual's concerns, I still had to be firm and say I was leaving at a certain time to get a moped that I'd organised to zoom me off to where Lewis would be. This individual certainly knows broadcasting, whereas I'm still learning about it, but I'm business savvy enough to know that me doing the podium interview with Lewis Hamilton just having won his fourth world title was absolutely the right thing for our broadcast. Nonetheless, I still felt it was correct to respect his experience and position, even though ultimately I had to do it my way. So going back to my point, for your team structure to work and function productively, you've got to respect the chain of command. You have to listen and respect the views of people in your company – don't just dismiss them out of hand if you don't agree.

Another central part of building a winning team is how that culture responds when something goes wrong, when there is a crisis or a failure. It's fantastic when everything is going great, when success follows success, but what happens to a great team when dark times arrive? Suddenly the question becomes, how do you maintain motivation, keep on pushing as hard as before, when you know that you are working in the face of some major challenges – quite often not even of your own making? Earlier I mentioned Sir Frank Williams' astonishing recovery from his appalling car accident; well, behind that personal triumph is a remarkable tale of a winning team responding to a severe crisis in the most amazing way possible. The incredible success of the Williams F1 team in the wake of Frank's terrible accident is one very famous example of a team coming together during a crisis to deliver elite success. In my opinion, this must rank as one of the great Formula 1 achievements. Frank was the driving force behind Williams, and that road accident in 1986 threatened the team's very existence. At least, that's what many people thought. However, despite Frank being hospitalised and on the brink of death, his team knuckled down without him, Patrick Head stepped into the leadership role supported by the likes of Sheridan Thynne, the commercial director, and Peter Windsor, the team manager. In some ways, the fact that the season had just begun was a good thing, because the team was already a well-oiled machine, and drivers Nelson Piquet and Nigel Mansell were at the top of their game in the Williams-Hondas. Incredibly, as I mentioned, Frank was out of hospital and able to visit the team within a couple of months, his first race visit being at the British Grand Prix in mid-July – where he was warmly welcomed back by the entire paddock. Perhaps most astonishingly of all, the team went on to comfortably win the Formula 1 World Championship for Constructors, and was only narrowly beaten in the World Championship for Drivers by McLaren's Alain Prost, Mansell finishing two points behind him, and Piquet one point behind Mansell.

The major takeaway from this period in Williams' history illustrates the importance of building a robust organisation that can sustain its performance even when hit by a crisis, in this case a tragedy involving the founding partner. The organisational structure was in place to continue without Frank, demonstrating that he had the right people around him, the best talent available in the key technical, operation and commercial roles. The team and the structure were far more capable than any one person, even Frank.

The team did not miss a beat, which meant everyone knew what was expected of them, and there was genuine alignment around the goals that Frank and Patrick had set that year. Everyone was able to put their heads down and plough on; they had all clearly bought into the team vision and goals. In some ways the accident can be said to have energised the team into doing everything it could 'for Frank'.

With regards to my own story, being promoted to race driver in the aftermath of Senna's death gave me a first-hand insight into how a great team works under intense pressure in the midst of a crisis. We all had to work through a very emotional time, pulling together as a team, staying focused, relying on each other even more than we did normally. For me, as the new, young driver, it was not an easy journey, but the team really closed around me, gave me all the support they could, and stuck to their well-proven systems. Because they were already a strong team, which was used to working together in a very collaborative way, that protected everyone in a time of great stress and enabled Williams F1 and all its people to recover. That is a top team at work.

I can't write about Formula 1 and teamwork in 2018 without talking about the remarkable recent dominance of Mercedes. I haven't been involved in that success story in the way I have been with McLaren, Williams or Red Bull, but it is clear for all to see what an incredible team they have built. There is a lot of discussion in the media analysing the extent of Mercedes' dominance, but I can share with you that the only way they have achieved this phenomenal level of performance is to have worked extremely hard since they took over that team in 2010 and spent four years developing its potential. During that time they were often being beaten – 2010–2013 were Red Bull Racing's dominant seasons – but Mercedes had a plan, and they stuck to it.

My old rival (and friend) Michael Schumacher played a part in that plan, and he came out of retirement to spend three years working alongside Nico Rosberg, helping Mercedes to evolve their product and technology, while also building that team into a formidable force. In addition, they invested a lot of money into innovating new technologies, particularly around the new hybrid engines which were introduced for the 2014 season.

We have seen the fruits of Mercedes' hard work both in the Formula 1 team, but also in their engine division in Brixworth, with more than 1,500 people working together to bring the World Championship titles across those dominant years. Every single one of those people has played an important part in Mercedes' success.

We also can't talk about teamwork without mentioning McLaren, one of the most successful F1 teams of all time. As you know, I drove for McLaren for nine years and during that time won 12 of the 13 Grands Prix victories on my CV. McLaren was a highly focused team, with strong processes geared towards winning, and just like Red Bull and Williams, every level of the business was involved in making sure it did its part in guaranteeing success. McLaren had a great leader in Ron Dennis, a precise and structured culture and very clear goals, plus some of the finest F1 minds you will ever come across.

Teamwork and collaboration lie at the heart of every successful Formula 1 project. In spite of all of the cutting-edge technology involved in the sport, the reality is that getting people to work together towards a common goal, often when under intense pressure, takes up a great deal of time and effort on the part of leadership teams. We often see high-profile partnerships in Formula 1 fail to deliver success, and when you look at these examples there is frequently a perceived technological failure, but actually the root cause often comes down to a failure of people, teamwork, communication and culture.

Ultimately, getting the most from a group of people to create a winning team is one of the biggest challenges we face in sport and in business. It is not easy, otherwise everyone would do it. Red Bull have excelled at that, so have teams such as Mercedes, McLaren and Williams. If you are very clear about your own personal targets and objectives and have a strategy for achieving that, then creating a winning team around you will be one of the most rewarding, productive and energising experiences you will ever have.

· · ·

To close this chapter, I'd like to illustrate all these inter-related elements of creating a winning team by looking at the incredible art of Formula 1 pit stops. One of the most crucial parts of a Grand Prix that decides track position – and therefore results – is when the car is not moving. Making sure the car is stationary for the shortest space of time possible can make the difference between winning or losing a race. I've certainly won Grands Prix because my pit-stop crew have done a better job than another team's and got me out in front. At the 1997 Italian Grand Prix, for example, I came in to the pits behind Jean Alesi, but I went out of the pits in front of him and won the race. That victory was solely down to fantastic teamwork. My contribution was literally delivering the car to a pit box and then the brilliant servicing of those people absolutely played a massive part in that win.

We have around 20 mechanics per car in the team to service two cars during a Grand Prix weekend. Of these, 20 also act as the crew during the all-important pit stops which we have during the race to change the four wheels and tyres, adjust the aerodynamics and also carry out any repairs, such as when we damage a front wing or nose section. The mechanics do a lot more than build the car to the right specification, they also have to deliver a service – call it customer service – to me during the race. That team is very tight-knit, there is a strong sense of interdependence; we work together to win together, lose together, and be safe together.

You have to ask yourself: if you'd been rude to that pit crew the week before, are you sure they will be 100 per cent committed to your tyre change? Most will likely still be committed, because they can separate their emotions and deliver their job, but what if there is one guy who did take offence, who remembered that you paid him no attention or respect a few days ago at the factory, maybe he is even thinking about that as you pit… that's how mistakes can be made or focus lost. In a world where margins are measured in tenths of a second or less, anything other than full commitment and focus will not give you the win. If that happens, is it really the pit crew's fault? Or are you partly to blame for your failure to engage with that person days earlier?

When I started racing in Formula 1, pit stops took six seconds or more, which was very impressive considering that we not only changed the wheels and tyres, but refuelled the cars as well. The refuelling equipment delivered the fuel at ten litres per second, and usually we took on around 60 litres on each stop. It was inherently dangerous, as Jos Verstappen found out at Hockenheim in 1994 when his car exploded in a ball of flames, so we had to manage that. Refuelling was later banned and immediately the top teams saw an opportunity to improve pit-stop times to less than six seconds.

As the driver, I have to come into the pits at the right time, being sure not to lose too much speed on the 'in' lap, and then bring the car to a halt in the pit box exactly where the team is waiting. Waiting for me is a team of well-drilled mechanics about to do something really extraordinary: perform a pit stop during which all four wheels and tyres are changed, and the aerodynamics of the car adjusted in less than *three* seconds.

Every single member of the team knows precisely what they have to do, taking responsibility and knowing that they are fully accountable. They have a fixed set of processes to follow using equipment and technology provided by the team to give them the best chance of success, and they know that performance and safety are paramount.

You really don't want to be the mechanic who drops the wheel nut and watches as it rolls across the pit lane, or fumbles with the wheel gun while trying to remove the wheel. Meanwhile, I'm sitting in the car looking at you, wondering why I am losing valuable places in the race, not to mention the fact that the team is in full view of the world's media and millions of television viewers.

Think about the task facing the crew.

Two are required to operate the front and rear jacks. The front jack man is standing in the pit lane waiting for me to go from 200mph to 50mph in the pit lane then stop at his feet so that he can slide the specially designed jack under the centre of the front wing and lever the car into the air. The front jack has to be located precisely, engaged positively with the car and activate instantly.

The same front jack man must then watch as his colleagues perform their tasks and when they are completed, hands raised to signal that their jobs are done, be ready to drop the car back onto the ground and step out of the way, removing the jack from the path of the car to enable it to power its way back down the pit lane.

The rear jack is engaged as soon as the car is stopped and, since the operator has to wait for the car to enter the pit-stop box, comes a fraction of a second after the front jack has been engaged. The rear of the car carries most of the weight, including the engine and gearbox, and once it is levered into the air the two rear wheels, larger in size than the front, can be slipped off and replaced.

The rear jack man has to wait until he sees the rear wheels have been fully located on their hubs, the wheel men moving back, before he can drop the car onto the ground. For the rear jack man there is the added complication that the rear wheels are used to transfer the 900bhp produced by the engine to the track, so it's vital that the wheels are back on the ground before the driver drops the clutch and wheel-spins his way into the pit lane. Dropping the car onto the ground with the wheels spinning can be a recipe for disaster.

Then we have two personnel whose job it is to stabilise the car which, balancing on centrally mounted jacks front and rear, can be in danger of rocking towards either side. They step forward, grab the central roll hoop, watching their colleagues changing the wheels before stepping aside as the jack men drop the car back to the ground.

Each wheel requires three personnel. One to use the wheel gun to remove the wheel nut and then drill it back on, while the other two remove the wheel and replace it with a new one. The wheel guns are heavy, the wheels and tyres weigh nine kilos, and these guys are under a lot of pressure.

These three technicians have four tasks to perform inside three seconds; wheel nut off, old wheel off, new wheel on, wheel nut on. That works out at 0.75s per task. When people talk about split second teamwork, this is it in action.

When you multiply that operation by four, you have 12 personnel each facing the same extraordinary challenge. For those working in the most competitive teams in Formula 1, they go to work on these pit stops knowing that their performance really will make the difference between winning and losing.

Finally, we have the crew responsible for making small aerodynamic adjustments. This is carried out by means of quick-release mechanisms on the front wing flaps which allow for the angle of the wing to be increased or decreased, while on the rear wing a 'Gurney' flap, which is a long thin vertical addition to a typical wing, can be altered and even removed entirely. Again, as with the wheel change, the time frame is three seconds.

In F1 the competition quickly catches up so you can never be complacent – through adhering to all of the core ideas about a winning team that I have talked about in this chapter, all the major teams can now consistently achieve a pit stop in between 2 and 2.5 seconds; the leading pit crews are managing to achieve 1.7 and 1.8 seconds during practice. In that time, the 20-man crew has 36 tasks to perform.

Now *THAT* is teamwork.

CHAPTER 5
MARGINAL GAINS

When I often say that I was not *the* best racing driver, various people tell me that I'm too hard on myself, reminding me of all the races that I won and the challenging moments when I did well. I get that, I know all those facts (luckily I was there), but the history books don't lie, the records don't show me as a Formula 1 World Champion. So, either I am the unluckiest Scot from the south-west of Scotland, or I'm the luckiest Scot from the south-west of Scotland!

When I retired, I held the record for the most Grands Prix competed in by a British driver (246), had scored the most career points (535) and had 13 wins to my credit. I'm obviously very proud of that. At one point I was also the fifth most winningest driver in F1, but what I will say to you is this: who is the fifth fastest man in the history of the 100 metres? Do you know? I don't. I know that Usain Bolt is the fastest. Who is fifth in line to the throne? Who came fifth in the Premier League last season? We are increasingly in a world of ultimate delivery, when fifth is not good enough.

What I am essentially saying is that very good isn't good enough. Elite-level sport demands the exceptional. Same in elite business. In top-level sport, being very good will get you on the team but it won't keep you there. Exceptional performances combined with an incredible work ethic will always win over a high level of skill with no work ethic. Formula 1 is a world where only the exceptional is good enough. Anything less is considered, at best, disappointing. The stakes are high in Formula 1. Financially it is very big business, for sure. Plus, as I mentioned before, there is the undercurrent that serious injury or worse could happen if people do not do their job properly. This does demand a level of intolerance of the average, a dislike for 'just good enough'. I'm pretty sure Michael Schumacher never went to a race or test thinking, *I will aim to be good enough today*. You aim to be the best. First place. Top of the podium, not just somewhere in the points. That is how I judge myself, by those standards, that is the world which I have inhabited for much of my life and therefore those are the parameters by which I judge success. I had over 20 years of knowing that fifth was not even on the podium, so now I'm retired I don't want to run a company that is the fifth best at what it does. I want to be first.

Given what I said earlier about when you sign a (marriage) contract with a Formula 1 team, you also get the divorce papers ready at the same time, it follows that only the drivers who are constantly improving, evolving and bettering their performance will remain married to that team. The relationship always comes to an end. You have to be aware of that and therefore be prepared to evolve or die. There has to be growth. I managed to do that for nine years at McLaren, which I am very proud of; some driver's tenures at teams have been very much shorter!

So how do racing drivers ensure that they are constantly growing, evolving and staying ahead of their rivals? How does Formula 1 *constantly* evolve? How do these teams improve cars that are already perceived to be the very finest four-wheeled racing machines on the planet?

They do so by chasing *marginal gains* with an obsessive focus and relentless energy, in order to secure an edge over their competition.

Back in the 1950s, '60s and '70s, it was possible to introduce major innovations into Formula 1: mid-engined cars in the 1950s, wings in the 1960s, ground-effect aerodynamics in the 1970s and so on, but by the 1990s and 2000s the room for manoeuvre and significant leaps forward had been reduced by the FIA's strict rules and also the sheer amount of performance enhancement preceding that era.

However, the drive to beat rivals remained as fierce as ever, so teams had to look for gains that were necessarily smaller, but a gain nonetheless. Consequently, modern Formula 1 is a relentless quest for performance based on constantly reviewing, adapting and updating so that we have the best chance of success next time out. A driver, team or company that is growing and evolving generates a self-perpetuating momentum that can very quickly become almost unstoppable; by contrast, if a company or team is not evolving, that negativity and stagnant culture quickly suffocates the performance. This mentality of constant evolution has to come from the top but it also has to be something that is instilled in your team. You lead by your example, but if people are not appearing to be prepared to adapt and evolve, not motivated to want to improve, then they are probably not the right staff.

As I said, my view on marginal gains comes from being around the culture of F1. You frequently see a driver in a post-race interview who has done badly, saying, 'We need to look how we can change, this has to be improved…'; you will then see the racer who has won, but he will also most likely be saying, 'I can't stand still, the guys behind me are chasing hard, I have to push on.' Twenty-five years around that non-stop race to be the best has undoubtedly rubbed off on me. I can't think of any way to operate in business that doesn't involve growth and evolution. Every year during my racing career, I had to feel like I was a better version of myself – physically, mentally, in terms of application, knowledge, preparedness, focus – however slight the improvement, it was still a step forward. The minute you stop believing you're getting better, that's when you mentally retire and you're just making up the numbers – at that point there is a better version of you out there somewhere else in the world and you're in trouble, they will get the seat or the job, and deservedly so.

Look at the BlackBerry, look at Leicester City FC… there are countless examples of huge success followed by a failure to evolve. If you don't evolve the talent and ideas that got you to the top, then your unique advantage has been recognised and exploited and enhanced upon by someone else. That applies to any job, not just the top 20 F1 drivers or the top three racers on the podium.

So why are marginal gains so important in Formula 1 and what can you learn about that for your career or business? Well, the need to constantly develop, enhance and refine is what really separates the great from the good in Formula 1. Sometimes the team that wins the world titles might only have a very slight advantage, but that is all it took to lift the end-of-season trophy. To give you some context, each Formula 1 season sees the ten competing teams having to design a completely new racing car to a set of regulations defined by our sports governing body, the FIA; these set of rules focus on key aspects such as safety, the technologies and materials we are allowed to use, and innovations, which are an intrinsic part of our business.

Once you have designed, manufactured and started developing your car (no small feat), you then bring it to market, Formula 1-style, by quite literally racing head-to-head against the competition in 20 Grands Prix held across four continents from March through November each year. A winning team requires the combined efforts of hundreds of full-time staff and dozens of key technology partners who not only design and build these high performing products, but ensure that there is a process of relentless development across the season, a non-stop race for marginal gain.

Formula 1 is a highly regulated environment, rather like banking, which means that every entrant has to comply with the rules while at the same time scouring their plans to find areas of competitive advantage. As the rules have become ever more strict, it has become harder to innovate, or at least it has appeared to be difficult to innovate and find those marginal gains. Nonetheless, every tiny advantage found is priceless. For example, when you consider that my long-time competitor and former teammate Kimi Räikkönen won the 2012 Abu Dhabi Grand Prix by eight-tenths of a second, after one hour and 46 minutes of battling with the toughest racing competition in the world, you can understand that for a Formula 1 driver every single marginal gain is vitally important.

Clearly, one way that F1 teams achieve marginal gains is through innovation. Adrian Newey has often said that the tight regulations of recent years have stifled innovation. And yet Adrian and his team at Red Bull Racing have been among the best at finding ways to gain a slight advantage through innovation. Adrian reads the regulations in two ways: (1) understand what the regulations say, and (2) see what the regulations *don't* say, because those gaps are where you can find the opportunities to innovate. This does *not* mean that he is trying to cheat; it means that he is seeking to legitimately exploit all of the opportunities available to him.

One example of finding marginal gains through innovation was the cold-blown diffuser, and its successor, the hot-blown diffuser, deployed by Red Bull with the help of Renault in 2009 which resulted in four Championship titles. That single innovation helped Red Bull move to a level of performance that none of their rivals could easily match. That evolution gave them a marginal gain, a competitive edge.

Another example of the quest for finding a marginal edge over rivals came in the form of producing carbon-fibre wings which would change shape at speed: initially along their length, longitudinally, and later across their width, laterally. These apparently small changes in shape, caused by the airflow passing over the wings at speed, could provide valuable additional performance. It was not illegal, at least not illegal when it was developed, but eventually the FIA tightened the rules so as to make it impossible to use this approach.

However, when one door is closed, the teams just look else-where for marginal gains, however tiny they may seem. For example, teams also seek marginal gains by understanding how to generate additional kilos of downforce and this has resulted in the unending quest by aerodynamicists to add downforce while limiting drag. The car's aero is developed race by race with configurations of wing or bodywork designed to suit individual circuits, so as to gain a race-specific marginal advantage: for example, a low downforce configuration at Monza at one extreme as against the high downforce set up at Monaco or Hungary on the other. Those tens of kilos of downforce lead to tenths of seconds of performance gain. In Formula 1, that is an age.

Another key area is tyres and the way in which the four small contact patches (an oval shaped patch 305mm wide on the front, 405mm wide at the rear, although this will vary depending on tyre pressure/loads) reacts with the track can be used to optimise the mechanical grip, communicate steering input and generate traction under acceleration or braking. Attention to detail in regard to how the tyres are used, such as the pressures they run, the surface temperature and so on, is vital, a small change in tyre behaviour will have a huge impact on overall performance. Marginal gains once more.

It's worth pointing out that for the drivers, this constant gain in performance comes with its own challenges in terms of keeping up with the progression. For example, at the start of my career I drove a conventional steering wheel with one button yet, by the end, the steering wheels were state-of-the-art pieces of technology with 35-plus buttons and an LCD screen that could display 100 pages of data systems. So I was always aware that evolving my own knowledge to keep up with the fast-paced growth of F1 tech was crucial and this sheds light on how business should look to improve, every lap, every session, every practice, every race. Had I not learnt how to use those various generations of ever-more complex steering wheels, my career would have been over very quickly.

Getting back to the teams' pursuit of marginal gains, let's drill down even more specifically. They all strive for gains at every race weekend, in the most minute fashion. They break down each race into stints, then each stint into a series of laps, then each lap into performance across three sectors and finally each sector into a series of turns. They even break each turn into entry, mid-corner and exit, so that the driver working with his engineers can look at the data and seek to improve a specific corner entry braking, downshifting, turn in. We can then look at mid-corner performance in terms of the car's speed, angle, steering and trajectory before looking at how we exit, when we get on the throttle, straighten the steering wheel; it is all about finding small improvements. If you find one tenth of a second improvement against your rivals per lap – think about that, one tenth of a second – then after ten laps you have pulled away by one second. Over a typical Grand Prix race distance that could represent a gap of between five and seven seconds, which means you have won at a canter.

Using telemetry data, teams break each lap into milliseconds of information which means they can analyse precisely how the car is doing at every point around the track. Having deconstructed each lap into small details as above, they then look at what is needed to put together an optimal lap, discussing 'putting a lap together', which means driving each corner and sector in such a way that the driver sets personal bests and unleashes the best possible performance from the car.

As this point illustrates, aside from innovation, one of the key ways that F1 searches for these crucial marginal gains is by almost infinite analysis of data. Even if your career or business is not data-reliant, you can still learn from the level of detail that goes into F1's data analysis to inspire you to constantly analyse your own progress and evolution.

It's easy to say that teams analyse how the car performs in a particular corner; you hear the phrase, 'they've looked at the data' all the time, but what does that actually mean? When I was karting as a kid, I used to grade every single race. I had a little log book and when the race was over, I'd sit down in the motorhome writing down all the stats – fastest lap, position in the race, all the obvious stuff – but I'd also write down how certain corners felt, how many mistakes I made and where, how the kart performed, I even rated my performance on a scale of one to ten, and so on. Essentially, I was analysing my own data even as a kid. Interestingly, on reflection, I never gave myself ten out of ten; even if I won all the heats and the final, I always felt there was room for improvement!

In Formula 1, we practise the same principles only using multi-million-pound software and technology. It is absolutely critical that a team scrutinises its performance data. Every Formula 1 car has real-time telemetry, relaying large amounts of information to the engineering team about how all the systems are performing, including the driver. This means we can see precisely what is happening, and then make the right decisions aimed at optimising performance and managing risks. It is a data-driven environment in which we share information, and use this to help us make winning decisions.

Formula 1 is a data-driven business, so our starting point is to instrument the car with around 200 sensors which are monitoring, measuring and plotting all the key systems. The Electronic Control Unit on the engine, for example, has over 13,000 health parameters logged during a race, and all the data from the car is being transmitted real-time back to the technical team at the trackside and relayed back to Mission Control at our headquarters in the UK. Data has become the foundation of every tactical decision we make during a Grand Prix. There are a lot of variables to consider, and not all of them within our control. So we focus first of all on what we do know, such as the amount of fuel on board the car, as this affects weight and therefore overall speed, or on the degradation of the tyres, the track position and tactics being used by our competition, or the weather. A two-car Formula 1 team will generate 160 gigabytes of recorded data each weekend, and we have access to around ten terabytes of trackside storage. The data analysis engineers in a Formula 1 team are therefore crucial to helping translate what is happening to all the systems and give us a clear understanding of where the opportunities and challenges lie. They sit at the back of the garage, watching the data streaming from my car real-time as it goes around the track, with all the different parameters being shown on the screen. It's been estimated that 750 million numbers are transmitted from the car to the data systems during a Grand Prix – that's around twice the number of words each of us will speak in an average lifetime.

Most of the information is run-of-the-mill and tells us that everything is fine, so we spend a lot of time and energy looking for the data that tells us there is either an opportunity or a problem; better still, it helps us to anticipate a problem before it becomes serious and allows us to react accordingly. Again, this is where the team working together, sharing information, reacting swiftly and being completely focused on the target can create a marginal gain.

Other times, it is less about marginal gains and more about avoiding setbacks. Again, you don't need to be in a data-reliant business to understand the benefits of avoiding mishaps or setbacks. In any business, like F1, sometimes it is not possible to stop a problem developing, or find an immediate cure, such as when we suffer the failure of one of the gears in the gearbox, or a fault in a system, such as if the brakes start to overheat, which could lead to a catastrophic failure. But if the team can spot the problem, tell me on the radio and we agree a new tactic, for example not using that gear again or being easier on the brakes during the final laps of a race, it can make all the difference between winning and losing, or finishing the race versus retiring with mechanical failure.

From my perspective as the person driving the car, I am receiving information on the LED read-outs on my steering wheel, information from the pit-board which the mechanics show me on each lap to confirm my position, the gap to the car in front and behind, and other instructions. I am also being updated on the two-way radio link from my race engineer – maintaining communications is a critical part of being able to respond to the unexpected. As I am racing I am not only receiving and processing all this information but also driving the car according to the conditions, the race strategy and other factors, such as the behaviour of the competition. And I am constantly having to react, adjusting the car's attitude through corners, preparing for the next one. It's an incredibly demanding and dynamic environment, and nothing is ever the same from one lap to the next; you are constantly adapting to what is happening around you.

Regardless of all this on-board tech, as the driver I can only see the track directly in front of me, and maybe a little bit of the colour of the car behind me in my wing mirrors. Other than that, it's the steering wheel in my hands. So, the big picture of what is happening is actually not clear to me, because I am on my own, out on the race track, pedalling the car as fast as it will go, and my teammate will be doing the same things. Without the support of the team, the technology and our ability to use information real-time, it would be a very lonely experience. It puts some perspective into the early days of Formula 1 when such technologies had never been dreamt of and the drivers were very much on their own.

In F1, using data analysis to find room for improvement and marginal gain is painstaking. If you don't like annual performance reviews, just imagine what I have had to put up with during my 15-year career. With every tiny aspect of the car's performance being monitored real-time through those dozens of sensors, it means that every single thing I do as a driver is immediately visible to the team and is reviewed relentlessly and unforgivingly in minute detail, nano-second by nano-second.

It is the ultimate Big Brother system; in the old days, the drivers could tell little white lies about the car, make out that it was rubbish and claim that they were driving perfectly. By my era, that was impossible because if I braked half a meter too early or too late for a corner, shifted gear at the wrong time, put in too much or too little steering, or went off the track by a few centimetres, the team knew immediately. If you make a mistake, you are aware that by the time you get back to the pit lane the whole team will know. There is no room to hide. Admittedly, this kind of daily performance review is not for everyone, because most people do not like to admit their mistakes. But if you are serious, ambitious and determined to achieve the very best results possible, then every aspect of performance has to be scrutinised, reviewed and improved daily. It's not about blaming people, it is simply about understanding how to get the best performance out of our team. Marginal gains do not come from ignoring problems, mistakes or poor performance.

The search for marginal gain through data analysis does not stop when the chequered flag falls. Each driver fulfils their FIA media obligations and then heads immediately into a lengthy and exhaustive debrief. This is standard practice. The debrief with the team includes the engineers, technicians and key suppliers, typically a room containing around 20 key people, all wearing headsets, linked up by ISDN to all the key engineers and technical experts back at Mission Control (in the case of Red Bull Racing, in Milton Keynes). This is while some of the crowd are still dispersing, with the dust on the Grand Prix hardly settled.

That team of people will then go through the minute detail of how the race unfolded. How was the start, any issues? Any suggestions to improve that? Any development ideas that will assist? Or was it a driver issue that I can work on? The start is only a few seconds but they will pore over that single moment for some time. Then the same process of examination will be applied to the entire race, regardless of how long that takes. These meetings can sometimes last as long as a couple of hours, depending on how eventful or challenging the race has been (although I've heard of some that have only lasted five minutes because a driver has walked out!). Typically, though, these debriefs are around an hour or so. And there are no exceptions to this rule: I recall when Sebastian Vettel won his first World Championship in Suzuka in Japan in 2010, most people expected to see him immediately partying hard into the night –

especially when you consider Red Bull's tradition for having some of the best celebrations in F1 – but in fact after he finished the podium celebrations, did the press conference and media interviews, Seb then went straight into a technical debrief so that the team could look at every aspect of that race, see where they could have done better, look at areas of weakness or concern, and keep the focus on developing into the future. This is not uncommon – I may have won a race by five seconds, but could I have won it by 20 seconds? Were my pit stops optimised, was there anything that didn't work absolutely perfectly? These debriefs are exhaustive and hugely valuable and are a part and parcel of every F1 team's working life. Maybe something similar could be part of your working life?

During my entire F1 career, I raced in 246 Grands Prix. When you consider that I probably spent six hours each weekend in technical debriefs looking at information, that means that in my 15-year career as a Formula 1 driver I spent well over 450 hours driving a Formula 1 car in a race but over 1500 hours looking at data and talking about it!

Everyone in the team debrief has got access to the same data, linked up to a server so they can all be looking at the same details simultaneously. Sometimes it won't be a discussion in terms of hard data, or ones and zeros or a nice pretty coloured graph which tells you if the performance went up or down; sometimes it will be what I call 'emotional data'. The driver might say, 'Okay, we won this one, but I have this feeling that something wasn't right here…' and he will try to explain what that feeling is. This is where the value of the team really kicks in, because if it isn't hard data, then his teammates have to intuitively know what he is concerned about, they have to be able to read and understand his concerns, even though there isn't necessarily any data to back that up, and find the problem and offer a solution.

The debrief is critical because it produces the most important output on our performance of the weekend, a report taking an overall view of all the systems, the processes and the people. Everyone hears first-hand what the problems are, even if you have just won the race, because you know the competition are working just as hard to emulate your success and try to beat you next time out. You want to learn as much as possible so that you adapt and evolve. The process is designed to highlight any issues that could have been what is called 'mission critical'. We use the momentum, emotion and immediacy of the race to download all the key feedback; there is no leaving that meeting until we get agreement on the key takeaways. This is especially true if there has been a problem, because the sense of urgency has to be maintained in order to get things resolved before the next race – which might be the following weekend, and therefore only four days away.

The way F1 teams analyse the data in these debriefs is meticulous. In motorsport, it is often (wrongly) assumed that because a lap time is quicker then the car must be quicker. Naturally a lot of drivers attach an awful lot of emotional importance to the lap time. However, it does not necessarily concur that the car is quicker just because the lap time says so. In actual fact, it may be the circuit has evolved or you have got a new set of tyres or perhaps the brakes were too cold before. So the car isn't actually physically better but the potential has been improved because of an external factor. If you think about it, if you credit the tyres but in fact it was just the ambient track temperature, then you're misleading yourself. You need to be aware and sure of where your marginal gain has come from – it doesn't matter if it was presented by innovation, data or otherwise, be sure you know where the gain originates from.

In F1, data tells us the truth about our performance. If you want to evolve and constantly improve, if you want to find those marginal gains, data is your friend, even if you sometimes think it isn't. The reason we are so reliant on data is that a Formula 1 car is designed and developed on the basis of information, and its entire configuration defined back in a factory using a combination of technologies including computer-aided design, computational fluid dynamics, finite element analysis and so on, and tested using both sophisticated computer modelling and physical checking of its aerodynamics in a wind tunnel.

A Formula 1 car is less like a car and more like an aircraft; in fact, it's essentially like a jet fighter that is designed to fly down instead of up! And rather like a pilot who might find it difficult flying across the ocean by himself, as an F1 driver I am rather reliant on having the best technology and systems at my disposal in order to be able to do my job.

The aerodynamic configuration of an F1 car is unique, exquisite in design, and is the result of many months of work by people using systems that give them the raw information needed to optimise the design. We are aiming to produce something like 5G – that's five times the force of gravity – through the corners, and 6G under braking – which feels like someone hitting you on the back of the head with a sledgehammer! We will be generating over two tonnes of aerodynamic downforce from a car which these days, with a driver sitting in it, weighs a total of just over 700 kilos.

So, when we finally build the car and take it to a race track we want to ensure that the car is behaving as we expected it to, reviewing the performance of all the systems and trying to make sure that there is a correlation between what we developed at the factory and what is happening on the race track. If we aren't getting the outcome we expected, if there's an issue which we need to understand, looking at the data and combining it with the knowledge within the team and my feedback as a driver will usually help us understand what the problem is.

If you find a weakness in the car, then you know how to remedy that. Perhaps a front brake was close to overheating. If that happens, that is indeed mission critical. So you have to create more cooling for the next time. The knock-on effect of more cooling is more drag. So what effect does the improved cooling idea have on aerodynamics? There is always a consequence to everything downstream; it's like dropping a pebble into a pond and then seeing the ripples flow out to the bank and rebound. Every business is the same, you need to observe your failings and weaknesses, analyse them in tiny detail, find a remedy then carefully plot the implementation of that remedy out so that you are fully aware of all the implications for every area of the business and armed with enough information to make marginal gains.

Do not be afraid of technology and data. The information technology revolution has had a profound effect in helping us to unleash performance and manage risk, giving us access to better information, helping us to build smarter systems and ultimately to give our businesses the competitive edge in a race.

Having said all of this, championing data and technology as I have, you mustn't underestimate human input in terms of finding marginal gains. I mentioned earlier about using your gut instinct, and also how 'emotional data' can be crucial. Some of the most significant decisions a team makes after a race come from the driver 'sensing' a problem or area for improvement. I am not a designer, but what I can do is explain to my team the issues that are stopping me from going faster on track. They might have the theory, but I have to deliver in practice. It's all very well some engineer telling me that the car should take a sixth-gear corner at 180mph, but I am the team member who has to go out and do it! Sometimes that is just a driver's instinct and no amount of computer data will convince me otherwise. In those cases, I have to believe in my ability and instinct and put that case forward. The same should apply to your business: do not reduce it to just a series of ones and zeros. Data cannot teach you everything.

The relentless pursuit of marginal gains should also never exclude learning from others around you. Let me use Alain Prost as an example. When I was a young racing driver on my way up the ladder, looking into a Formula 1 team from the outside and watching all these famous racers, these incredible champions appeared to be almost other-worldly figures with all their achievements and legendary races behind them. However, once I actually joined a team, they were suddenly my teammates and work colleagues and I was around them almost every day. They were no longer untouchable, they were just like me. I always found that this was the moment when I could really observe and learn so much, up close. I tried not to be intimidated and to just see this as an amazing opportunity to watch these champions at work and soak up what they do.

I've previously referred to the next story as a 'pinch me' moment. What happened was, as a Williams test driver, I had just arrived back in the garage and was waiting in the car for the next test session. I was only 22 years old. I looked across and sitting in the other car was The Professor, Alain Prost. When Prost joined Williams in 1993 he was a huge star, a four-time world champion and one of my biggest inspirations; in fact, I'd say I looked up to him more than any other racer. Like myself and so many other F1 drivers, Prost had come to the attention of the motorsport community by winning a number of international kart championships in the 1970s followed by a dominant phase in Formula 3. A move to Formula 1 soon followed, debuting for McLaren in 1980 before moving to Renault then on to McLaren (recently taken over by Ron Dennis, where Prost would initially be paired with Niki Lauda, and later in a strained partnership with Ayrton Senna), where he would win titles in 1985, 1986 and 1989. He would win his fourth world title with Williams after two seasons at Ferrari. By the time I met him in that garage, Prost was a racing legend, famous for his highly analytical approach paired with a smooth, unflustered driving style which was deceptively quick.

For me, sitting there looking at him in that Williams garage, it felt like a real privilege and a big moment. After I'd got over the fanboy moment, I knew this was the first of many opportunities to learn so much. Just listening to him, the answers he gave, the questions he asked, his body language, his demeanour, I just tried to soak it all up. Of course, the data we had available back then was far less than in the modern sport, but nonetheless there was technology at hand. I felt that being around drivers such as Prost was the most fantastic way to make sure I personally kept evolving, learning, improving, in order to find those marginal gains.

There will no doubt be someone you work with who might be similar, maybe a senior executive or a manager you admire; just make sure that when you are working with them closely, you are learning. You don't necessarily need to grill them for advice, sometimes just watching is enough. They might teach you some of the most important lessons you will ever learn. And to evolve you always have to learn.

Taking all these approaches into consideration, Lewis Hamilton is a great example of someone who searches out marginal gains. At the time of writing, he has just won his fourth world championship. You don't do that if you are not constantly evolving. He has clearly worked on the weaker parts of his driving. For example, he has always been an incredible racer, able to extract the very best out of himself and his car in the white heat of the battle on track. However, his qualifying did not always match that brilliance. So, for example, in 2014 his rival and teammate Nico Rosberg frequently out-qualified him, 11 times out of 19 races, in fact. Lewis responded to this, focusing on making marginal improvements needed during a single-lap qualifying session and was therefore able to dominate his teammate by return the following year, outperforming Rosberg 12 times out of 19. He also applied the same approach to his starts: Nico's 2016 season was superior for faster starts so Lewis worked in the simulator to improve his clutch operation and did indeed turn his starting technique around for the better. The fact that Lewis is still improving – and still *looking* to improve – is one of the reasons why he is so difficult to beat. He understands the benefit of marginal gains and how that can lead to him having the competitive edge. And let's be honest, it's worked!

• • •

By way of a final illustration, I'm going to highlight the process of searching out marginal gains by deliberately revisiting those remarkable people who do F1 pit stops. I've already detailed the level of teamwork in a top pit crew so it makes sense to expand on that foundation and use them to also show that marginal gains can always be found, even at the very elite level of any sport or business. Hopefully this might provide an inspiration for the same search for improvement in your career or business.

In 2011 Ferrari became the first Formula 1 team to execute a pit stop in three seconds when they achieved this remarkable feat for Fernando Alonso at the Korean Grand Prix. Three seconds is less time than it takes to read that sentence. The Ferrari pit team had worked on this for a number of months, getting the mechanics themselves to work on the technology and processes until they were confident of being able to deliver it under pressure. A pit stop is over so quickly that it is hard to appreciate the amount of effort and detail that has gone into being able to do that, time after time, all under immense pressure during a fierce F1 race. In so doing,

Ferrari were able to secure tangible marginal gains when Alonso's car was stationary.

The amazing thing is that when the mechanics at Red Bull saw Ferrari managing to do this pit stop in three seconds, they were able to not only work out what Ferrari were doing, but then develop their own marginally better systems, processes and technology in order to beat them. After an immense amount of analysis and then hard work, in 2013 the Red Bull team was able to replace all four wheels and tyres on Mark Webber's car on lap 28 of the United States Grand Prix in a remarkable 1.92 seconds!

You might think that this sub-two-second time was unassailable. However, that's not how Formula 1 works – constant evolution through marginal gains, remember – so the story does not quite end there. My first team at Williams saw the progress made by Red Bull and benchmarked their performance against it. By analysing all the data, both from their own performances and those of their competitors each and every weekend, retraining staff, rebuilding the process and challenging established methods, by 2016 the Williams team was consistently the best pit crew in Formula 1. At the Azerbaijan Grand Prix in Baku in 2016 they set a new world record for Formula 1 pit stops. Although the timing monitors showed 1.92 seconds (which is the same as Red Bull Racing), the Williams car was static for only 1.89 seconds. To think that 25 seconds used to be regarded as a decent pit stop in the 1980s – that is some evolution!

So, one of the biggest lessons to draw from motorsport is that it's constantly looking for an upward trajectory in performance, for what can come next. You learn this from a very young age. Way back when I was in karting as a kid, my father would go, 'Why are you looking behind you?' I told him I was looking to see where my competition was. He replied, 'Well, as long as they are behind you, that's all you need to know. Look forward, look to where you are going. Don't look at where you've been.' It's always been about moving forward, progression, evolution.

Formula 1 teams and drivers are *never* satisfied with how they are performing. There is always more to come. Marginal gains can always be found if hard work, innovation, data and human input are used to improve results. Formula 1, just like your career or business, is a race without end.

CHAPTER 6
ATTENTION TO DETAIL

Closely aligned to both marginal gains and unleashing your personal potential is absolute attention to detail. So many elements of your job and career require focus that sometimes there is a risk of letting your attention to the small detail stray, but if you do that things can quickly fall apart. The top achievers, the elite performers, the leading business people keep paying close attention to detail.

One Formula 1 driver who is famous for his complete and meticulous attitude is Sir Jackie Stewart. As I mentioned earlier, aged just 17, I found myself racing in Formula Ford and it was during that period that I received the unexpected phone call from Jackie (the one I initially suspected was a wind-up by my mates). Fortunately, it wasn't a prank call and instead led to that incredible opportunity for me to drive with Paul Stewart Racing; as I have explained there were good races and bad during my time with that team, but being around Sir Jackie was always the most remarkable experience.

Clearly being mentored by Sir Jackie in terms of racing was a massive experience and learning curve. However, it was also absolutely fascinating watching and learning from him away from the track, seeing how he handled himself in life and in business. Jackie has always said, 'Being in elite sports gives you an unfair advantage in business', an idea I will come back to later in this book. For the purposes of this chapter, Jackie was all about two things: attention to detail and delivering.

For example, Jackie was really into how you dress, how you present yourself. He sent all his drivers to Lee Bowman at the Kingstree Group in London, who worked with prime ministers, politicians and captains of industry to help them with their personal presentation, speeches and so on. I have to be honest and say I really didn't enjoy that process at all. However, I did learn a lot; to be fair, my parents had always told me about the importance of presentation, being polite, dressing properly, but what Jackie did was put even more energy and structure into that in terms of being a racing driver.

One time when I was racing for Sir Jackie in Formula Three, I turned up slightly late for an appearance with a Ford guest in a box at Silverstone. I might have been five minutes late or whatever, but immediately after the event Jackie told me that I should write a letter to the senior person at Ford. I remember the exact words he used: 'I would like to apologise for the slight glitch', which at the time seemed like a weird thing to say. I did what he asked and apologised in writing for the slight glitch in my arrival time, explaining that I had been with my engineers and focused on the race and slightly lost track of time for five minutes. I printed the letter out, signed it and posted it (none of this emailing!). Now, no doubt the recipient opened that letter, read it quickly, thought, *That was nice of him to say that*, and threw it in the bin. That's not the point; it was all about the follow-up, acknowledging I had been very slightly late, making the client aware that I would normally not be tardy, that I knew the importance of punctuality, and so on. So that little letter might have just been a few lines long but was saying so very much more. Jackie applied that level of detail to *every single element* of his business and his racing. That is pretty exhausting if you think about it, but he never wavered. Still doesn't.

To this day, Jackie will still earn more each year than the majority of the grid with his brand contracts and business involvement and that is not by chance. In recent years, he brought both Heineken and Rolex into Formula 1, he previously enjoyed long-standing brand ambassadorships with big companies such as Ford and Goodyear. Jackie retired as a Grand Prix driver in 1973 but is as switched on now as ever. A large part of that is down to his legendary personal brand, attention to detail and delivery.

Jackie's energy and brand awareness are revered and renowned. Look at him today. He is in his seventies, yet he still walks around in tartan trousers and the flat cap, keeping true to his brand. In fact,

I think he stands out in the paddock as much as Lewis Hamilton, despite having retired over 40 years ago. People might recognise Lewis because he is current, and maybe some of the younger ones might not recognise Jackie or not be aware of his many achievements, but they will know he is a man and a presence to be remembered.

Very early on in my television career, I was told that it is 70 per cent what people see and 30 per cent what you say. Similarly, I read a study somewhere that suggested that when you are watching the weather forecast, you are partly watching the clouds and the wind patterns, but you are also watching how the weatherperson is dressed and how they present the forecast. Jackie knew these facts decades ago.

Clearly, Jackie had a big influence on me in many ways, but for the purposes of this chapter his obsessive attention to detail rubbed off on me very much in my young life and racing career. For example, I decided very early on that if I could be on the smarter side of personal presentation, I would. So very often I will wear a sports jacket even it's really hot because, let's be honest, it hides your sweat marks! Also it just looks smarter.

This brings us on to the topic of first impressions, which is clearly affected by your attention to detail. We've all been told since we were little that we should never judge a book by its cover. I have a friend who is an internationally successful author and let's just say he does not follow the Jackie Stewart school of immaculate presentation, in fact, he's been turned away from his own book events. Yet he is at the very top of his game and says that because he spends most of his life alone, writing, he doesn't need to wear smart clothes.

It's all about perception. In business, that can be a very powerful ally but also a very damaging enemy. I'm not suggesting that it always applies that the scruffy person is bad at their job, of course, not — my best-selling writer friend is a case in point. I'm just saying that as a general rule, people do *perceive* you differently depending on how you present yourself. Let's say you turn up to an expensive Harley Street doctor's surgery and the consultant is wearing ripped jeans and a white vest; he may well be the best surgeon in his field in the world, but your visual perception would probably convince you that he is not. Aircraft pilots are another simple example. Rightly or wrongly, I want to see the pilot of my aircraft standing there with his or her shoulders sagging under so many stripes. I have no idea what those stripes mean, but I want to see a lot of them!

In a perfect world, everyone is the same and everyone should have the same opportunity and potential and be judged purely on their performance rather than how they look; that would be wonderful and I'm all for it. However, rightly or wrongly, that is not actually how the real world operates.

I do get the argument about 'Why should I need to conform? My work should speak for itself.' I get that and I agree. However, I would simply counter that point by saying, 'Why swim against the tide?' You have only got so much energy in any given day. If you break it down to how many hours you are actually awake, creative and productive, why would you want to spend some of that time fighting against someone else's preconceptions of you because of the way you dress?

This approach to presentation extends to the people I work with. I find it odd when you go to a function and people from the event management team are wearing the same jackets and trousers but everyone has got their own choice of shoes on, some in sneakers, some in formal shoes, all different colours. I am a bit old school in that respect, I guess, maybe due to Jackie's influence and partly my upbringing, but in my opinion that just doesn't look as professional.

I get that in certain creative industries, such as with musicians and fashion designers, the accepted norms are often turned on their heads, so the less conventionally presented someone is, the more sense it makes in terms of their brand. Being different because it's sincere and represents who you are can be compelling. Essentially, though, that is the same argument in reverse – if I went to a punk rock gig in a beautifully tailored suit, then I'm sure a lot of people there would judge me by that look just the same.

So think about your presentation. Jackie wearing the tartan trousers might be something you've seen before, but if I ever hear a negative comment about that, I think it's just jealousy. Not necessarily jealous of the tartan, more just jealous of how Jackie has presented himself so precisely all these years. I've felt the benefit of his views on presentation many times – for example, he encouraged Heineken to use me as a brand ambassador, after which I thanked him and then asked if I should be doing something more concrete to show my appreciation, but he just said, 'No, I have my own contracts with them, I just think it is the right thing for them to use someone like you, because you present well.'

In the social media age, presentation is more important than ever. It's so easy to go on a review website, read some poor comments and immediately look elsewhere for your hotel or restaurant. That bad review might simply have come from a single bad first impression. Or like I said earlier, from the person on the desk at 5pm not having the engagement with the business to greet a visitor with a smile and a warm welcome. But that moment of lapsed presentation can spread very rapidly across social media and multiply incredibly quickly, becoming far more damaging than the single small incident could ever be in isolation.

The flipside of this discussion is that you need to have an awareness that presentation is not the only measure of someone's worth or talent. Yes, I choose to present in a smart suit but just because someone else doesn't never means that they are worth less. Take my writer friend, who doesn't even own a tie. He went to test-drive an expensive new car. When he got to the front desk of the dealership, he said, 'I'd like to talk to someone about your sports car please…' to which the receptionist looked him up and down quite deliberately and replied, 'Second-hand, I presume?'

How can that ever be good business? If he'd been wearing a Savile Row suit she would not have said that. Guess what? He didn't buy the car.

When my father went to business meetings he was always very smart, but day-to-day he was just in jeans and a jumper. On occasion when people walked into the office, they would look at him and say, 'Is the boss around?' and he would sometimes say, 'Oh yeah, I think he's out the back', and he'd send them on a long walk because they had just looked at him and made a judgement. That was at the office, behind the scenes if you like. For meetings he was always immaculate, so I think he had a good balance.

An amusing aside about Father is that he never wore a watch, yet he had the clock in his car set five minutes fast so that he was always on time. I remember pointing out that if he knew it was five minutes fast, how did it make any difference?… but he was not interested. It's funny because in our kitchen in Monaco we have the clock set five minutes fast because our son doesn't know the Coulthard family secret yet and it helps us get him to school on time! To be fair, I hate being late and that's probably no coincidence.

Of course, Jackie's famous attention to detail extends way beyond just how he dresses. Jackie is a classic example of how, in sport, you look into every detail because that's where there is potential to enhance and improve performance. Outside of sport, a lot of people don't look at the detail in the same way; they might *think* they do but they really don't, not compared to how a top sportsperson or team looks at the detail required to be the best in the world.

I am a big fan of attention to detail. I'm like Jackie and my father for that. I am aware it's bordering on slightly obsessive at times! I like things correct, neat and in order. I mentioned earlier that I used to clean the underside of my karts to make sure I knew that every single small piece was as it should be. My father provided me with the basic equipment but it was up to me to keep it clean and tidy. Plus if I ever flipped my kart in a crash, people would say, 'Crikey, that kart's got a clean floor!' That goes back to presentation. That little ritual with cleaning the kart really worked, because it gave me an appreciation of the amount of preparation needed before you can begin to achieve success. It is something I have carried with me ever since, and the only difference when I was winning races in Formula 1 is that the preparation involved many hundreds of people.

The second team I drove for in Formula 1 was McLaren. When I first arrived there, I was joining a team that, like Williams, had achieved significant successes over the years. What was different with McLaren was the fact that Ron Dennis was legendary for having an almost obsessive attention to detail. The cars were not only superbly engineered but brilliantly turned out. Ron is a unique individual. He spent his early career working as a technician for both the

Cooper and Brabham Formula 1 teams in the 1960s before starting his own team with partner Neil Trundle in 1971. More forays into team management and ownership eventually led him (along with his technical director John Barnard) to taking over McLaren when that team was struggling in the early 1980s.

From the outset, Ron rejuvenated McLaren, masterminding a trajectory that took the team to multiple World Championship-winning success with great drivers such as Niki Lauda, Alain Prost and Ayrton Senna. This included the feted 1988 season when the aforementioned McLaren MP4/4 won 15 out of 16 races. When asked how delighted he must be to achieve such a feat, Ron simply said that he was disappointed not to have won all 16.

Ron and his team were also absolute masterminds at recruiting commercial partners, so I was always acutely aware that I could learn so much more than just racing from him. Highly competitive, Ron's obsessive attention to detail is the stuff of Formula 1 legend, demanding of his team the very highest levels of presentation, preparation and performance. Ron has a very particular style, famous among the paddock, hugely precise, exacting and meticulous. Not everyone agrees with his management style and approach but Formula 1 records and the history books tell us that it works.

For example, Ron wanted us all to be clean-shaven and presented immaculately and that approach worked for me, all the cleanliness and everything, because that's how I was wired. Another time Ron had commissioned a building with gravel along the side. However, when it rained, the gravel was splashing dust up the side of the wall, so Ron told the company to remove the gravel, wash it all free of dust and then bring it back so that when it rained it didn't splash any more. I see nothing wrong with that – as much as I love the countryside, I do like the cleanliness of an apartment, a structured and organised life and environment. I was just lucky that I spent so much time at McLaren where Ron was constantly pushing for the same. His argument is that you wouldn't leave something untidy or lying around if you were working on an aircraft, so why would you do that when you are working on a racing car? I'm with Ron on that one. Ron may have taken it to the extreme sometimes, for example he didn't want drinks on the table or the desks, but I think his logic was perfectly reasonable and I was very much drawn to that. If you accept a cluttered environment then I think that tells people about the mind of the company, the DNA of the people working there; besides, cleanliness costs nothing, it's just an attitude. Ron's very particular mindset was right up my strasse.

This brings me on to the related topic of preparation. Just as you should apply attention to detail in your presentation and behaviour, then so too can you do the same with your preparation for a race, event, conference, important meeting, whatever. One of the biggest changes I have seen within Formula 1 has been the way in which we can replicate systems in a virtual environment so that we can develop and refine upgrades prior to bringing them into play at the race track, in the real world – essentially paying immense attention to detail in our pre-race preparation. This also applies to driver development, and nowadays it is commonplace for drivers to drive full-size simulators, rather like aircraft simulators, which allow them to learn complex systems and experiment with driving techniques in a safe environment, and without having to undertake public and very expensive track testing. It also has the added benefit of helping the drivers visualise and learn the race tracks before they have ever visited them, which is invaluable for both new drivers or when we have a new race track added to the calendar. This offers immense attention to detail in preparation. For example, Red Bull's six-axis simulator is state-of-the-art and allows the driver and team to evaluate many aspects of performance, from driver inputs through to looking at steering wheel functionality, systems operation and role-playing race scenarios. There is a misunderstanding about simulators: they are not there to teach you how to drive, they are there to familiarise you with systems and processes as well as improve the quality of decision making and evaluate potential changes to set-up. In a race you will make thousands of instant decisions governing performance and risk, and being prepared is key. We do not like surprises.

This attention to detail in preparation extends throughout the team. The engineering brains also use the simulation technology to run through hundreds of car set-ups and permutations which saves valuable time, and money, when the team arrives at a race track. Monte Carlo, which is a very twisty street circuit, has a very different car set-up compared to Monza in Italy, for example, which is made up of long, fast straights that place the emphasis on top speed and low downforce. Being prepared through simulation of the relevant set-up therefore allows the teams to start practice on a Friday morning in a much more efficient way, and then run through a pre-defined programme aimed at optimising the car's performance, both for the demands of ultra-fast qualifying and then the 200-mile Grand Prix itself.

As Jackie would teach you, it's all in the detail. For example, when I was racing, in qualifying during my era we ran with around 10 kilos of fuel on board, while at the start of the race we had 170 kilos, making the car around 30 per cent heavier. Considering that 10 kilos of fuel can cost up to three-tenths of a second in lap time on each and every lap, as the fuel load reduces so the performance of the car will improve. At the same time, however, the tyres will be degrading, their performance deteriorating over time, and this is heavily influenced by external variables including track temperature and the abrasiveness of the track surface.

So we have a constantly changing picture that is further affected by the car's track position relative to the opposition and other unforeseen events, such as accidents or weather changes. All these variables are being constantly reviewed to help us anticipate outcomes to increase our confidence and reduce risk. Without the attention to detail in our preparation, this would be much more tricky.

This approach doesn't just apply to car set-up, it is also highly relevant to new tech and upgrades as well as a host of other applications. Whether we are developing new hybrid power trains or looking for the next big improvement in design or technology, one of the most impressive changes I see within Formula 1 has been the way in which we build systems in a virtual environment. We can develop and refine upgrades prior to bringing them into play at the race track.

Why is this relevant to you in business? Because it is a prime example of F1 rehearsing and replicating real-world situations in advance, in minute detail, so that when the heat of battle commences, there are as few variables and unknowns as possible, the attention to detail in the preparation has maximised the chances of the car and team achieving their peak performance.

I would suggest that you don't just vaguely replicate circumstances of a forthcoming event. So, for instance, if you have a big presentation, then don't rehearse it in the comfort of your own living room, with the TV on in the background and the kids and dog running around. As far as possible, you need to replicate circumstances to accurately reflect the moment when you need to perform.

Let me give you an example from my own race days. There might be a circuit where we'd test and later race, and I'd perhaps go round super-fast first thing in the morning. However, as pleasing as that was, I knew that the race would be at 1pm, by which time the track and ambient temperatures might be different, there might be more or less wind, the tyres might be cooler, all sorts of factors could change. So I'd enjoy that moment of being quickest during early morning testing, but also realise that it didn't accurately reflect the race circumstances. There is an old motorsport saying that sums this up perfectly: the most important time to be quick is when it matters.

Another driver who I personally witnessed display great attention to detail and exacting preparedness in the paddock and on track was Ayrton Senna, in many people's minds *the* greatest of all time. I learnt so much from being around him. In 1994, I did my first test with him in Estoril for Williams. If I recall correctly, he did the first two days, then on the third day I was scheduled for a drive. I went in bright and early to the track only to find that Ayrton was already there. I assumed that if he was there then he must be testing, but I soon found out that I would still be driving and that Senna was there because he wanted to listen to what I was saying to the engineers and hear my feedback in the car. In effect, he was evaluating my performance, seeing if any small detail or snippet of a comment was made that might be of benefit, and no doubt giving Frank Williams feedback on how I was as a new member of the team. Fortunately, he was satisfied with the job I did, and as a young driver I really appreciated that.

However, the big takeaway for me that day was that even though Senna was already a three-time world champion, even though his time demands were considerably more than mine, he felt it was important to know whether this young Scottish racing driver was a good enough test driver for him to trust that the development of the car in testing would be done in a way that was acceptable.

That is impressive preparation and attention to detail. Now, it may not seem like much extra effort to stay over an extra night, come in and then listen for a while, but Ayrton could have been doing a million other things with his time at that point. Yet he wanted to know more about the car, about me, about the challenges of the season ahead. As an aside, I know from his manager, Julian Jacobi, that Ayrton was very complimentary about what he saw and heard, and he shared that opinion with Frank Williams – I'm sure that played a part in me getting the chance as a rookie to race for Williams (sadly when Ayrton was no longer with us for me to say thank you). I really appreciated his support and guidance as it fast-tracked my experience of where to look to improve overall performance; he was inspirational.

Getting back to the key point here, attention to detail in your preparation is everything. This has to then be followed up with total conviction. Once the day of the 'race' arrives, you have to go for it with the absolute belief and conviction that there is nothing more you can do, because you have exercised total attention to detail beforehand. That's why you prepare with absolute focus. Don't hope for a good result. Hope is not a strategy. You cannot go into battle hoping you will do well; you have to know you have done everything to give yourself the best chance. If you step on the field or get in a car or enter the business world believing your preparation is half-baked, believing you could have done more, then why on earth would you expect to be successful? Imagine if I had climbed into a 200mph car and went off on a hot lap with not enough preparation or focus. That lap is either going to be very slow or end up in the wall. Your next meeting or project might not be so precarious in terms of failure, but I do know the consequences of not preparing can be severe for all of us.

• • •

Attention to detail extends to every element of your personal brand, your job, company or career. One area which I think is sometimes disastrously overlooked is the social side of business and this can be where your personal brand can reap huge dividends. Formula 1 is brilliant for this because there are so many functions with rooms full of people in all sorts of businesses – a perfect opportunity to practise some attention to detail.

There was a period when I felt life was like one big series of cocktail parties. In fact, the title of my 2007 autobiography was at one point going to be *Life's A Cocktail Party*, because it just seemed that I was at one event after another, all the time. Although that is fun at first, it can become repetitive, especially the conversations.

However, I did learn some great skills and realised if I paid attention to these events and made a genuine effort with people, they could be hugely beneficial. The art of the cocktail party might seem quite superficial but in fact it is important for two reasons. Firstly, it is simply courteous and respectful to talk to people in a certain way and, secondly, you never know who you might meet. Even if the people going are familiar to you, social gatherings can be disarming and so acquaintances might behave differently and you may see them in a new light (hopefully not because they've had too much to drink!). So don't dismiss company events if they might offer you the chance to see and meet people in a different situation. So much in business is what happens in the bar or after the conference, where you start to get to know someone and build a relationship, you find common ground and comfort and trust and then that enables you to work so much better together.

Going back to my childhood in Twynholm, I learnt so much from my parents about building relationships at social gatherings. By the time I was heavily into karting, my family was reasonably well-off, Dad drove a nice Mercedes and as a family we were enjoying the benefits of all their years of hard work. However, more importantly, my parents were always what I call 'life rich'. Their extended family is very important to them and they have a cherished circle of friends, too. Their social skills and ability to get on with people was something I observed and then saw them replicate within their business. They really enjoyed the socialising aspect of business. Consequently, my father has built long-standing friendships within his world of work and that is crucial, in my opinion. They say 'Don't do business with friends', but in actual fact if, through business, you become friends then you have built a relationship that is much more likely to endure and even if for whatever reason the business opportunity runs its course, as friends you will understand.

If you graft as hard as my parents, then you spend a large part of your waking week at work, so if you are able to have fulfilling relationships with people you also consider friends, then that can only be of benefit to your enjoyment of the job and therefore, by association, your performance. I don't think people put enough time into building relationships. The old breaking of the bread and drinking of the wine that social interaction is, I think, a huge part of successful business. That is something that my mum and dad educated me about by example.

By the time I was an adult with a career in motorsport I realised one very entertaining fact at these events: Formula 1 is a cool calling card at a party when you are a young man; it's a pretty good conversation piece! Elite sport gifts you that profile, you don't have to make up small talk. 'What do you do?' 'I'm a Grand Prix driver.' That's your Top Trump card straight out the box! I really don't mean that in an arrogant way, but it is an answer that usually generates a lot of interest and conversation. To be fair, I have lived in that rather unreal celebrity bubble where a lot of people know your name, especially if I am at a motorsport weekend or conference. As I said earlier, even then I will always introduce myself as David. It's arrogant not to, isn't it?

However, back in the early days, my trainer at McLaren saw me at a lot of these parties and events and said that I needed to ask people more questions. I actually don't like to say, 'So what do you do?' because in my opinion that puts people in categories, in a box. Inevitably, some people decide when they hear, 'I am a bin man', that that person isn't useful or interesting enough and they glaze over. That's just plain disrespectful. Telling someone your job doesn't tell them anything about your hobbies or other stuff you're into. If someone says what do you do, I'd suggest replying with, 'I love running', or maybe 'I enjoy travelling to the Far East', or whatever it is you like. That will be a stimulus for a much more interesting conversation. Of course, there's always people at these parties and events who love the sound of their own voice, they like hearing their own name, and talking about themselves all night. That's unavoidable, but you don't necessarily have to listen to it all night.

It certainly makes a big impression if you treat people well and pay them attention and respect at social gatherings; that is good attention to detail. Equally, people remember if you do the opposite, which is clearly poor attention to detail. I was sitting at an event recently, next to a well-known celebrity and she was talking away and at one point she asked me a question. So I started answering her and halfway through she completely zoned out and was looking somewhere else. There was even a moment where she was not listening to a word I was saying but she still said, 'Yeah, yeah, yeah.' So I just stopped. I didn't take offence because I'm old enough to not worry about such things. But I will certainly remember that little incident.

One final point on functions, parties and networking: I know a lot of business manuals suggest you carefully take in someone's name and remember it; I'm not sure I'm that fussed about that, to me if you are clearly engaged in someone's conversation, then that is more of a compliment than remembering 60 different names in a room. I know this because I read it once in a study by... oh crikey, whatsisname?

. . .

You need to also pay attention to the atmosphere at work and within your team. It's no use if you only ever get along as a team when you've all had five pints and a curry. In business you have one big advantage over sport – you are not in business to entertain. As much as high-level sport is a competitive business, it is also a public one, so the millions of TV viewers and spectators on the day will simply switch off if what they are watching is not entertaining. That doesn't apply to a business deal.

However, that doesn't mean business should be boring. I like to make my business entertaining. I will be honest with you; if there is a room with 'sensible adults' in and also a few people who like a bit of fun or a giggle, I most definitely fall into the latter category. However, that is not a negative, it is because I believe you can get the job done and still have some fun. In fact, at times it is clear that having fun can alleviate some of the stress and tension and therefore make you more creative and productive. If there is a little joke to be made, why not? If that lightens the mood in a long meeting then how can that be a bad thing? I'm not suggesting you become some sort of joker that no one takes seriously, obviously, but if there's a choice between a fun, light-hearted but productive meeting versus a stern, serious one, I know which I'd rather be in. It will certainly make you and your employees look forward to work.

By building team spirit like this, you get people interacting with each other. It's not necessarily about taking them on an adventure weekend in a forest (which feels a bit forced although I'm sure it does work for some), but perhaps just a few Friday beers at the end of the week, to wind down to the weekend, reflecting on what has been going on that week, taking time to strengthen the friendships among the team. A lot of people don't take the time to do that, to build those relationships.

I've seen this with some of the racers I've come across, too. That master of attention to detail, Jackie Stewart, understands as much as any driver I know about the power of building relationships and sowing seeds today that may or may not be useful to you in the future. The risk of that approach is that cynics might view it as using people. I disagree strongly. The simple fact is that if you are sowing a seed because that person may be important in the future, in actual fact you are treating them with importance *today*, whether they prove to be important in the future or not. The key point is that you treat them well. If you work on the basis of treating everybody with respect, generally that cannot be a bad strategy, can it?

I'd like to make just a quick final point here about one tool that people use to establish and reinforce business relationships: corporate gifts. When I go to all these big business conferences around the world, they often give me shirts, hats, all sorts of gifts, even boxes of tea. Sometimes I have to leave them behind because I simply can't cart them all around the globe through airports. I feel bad about that, but I have learnt a lesson along the way. If I offer someone a gift in business, I make it something very special. For example, I mentioned ealier how I gave Dietrich Mateschitz, owner of Red Bull, a Theo Fennel replica of a Red Bull Can that I'd had made in silver with no lid, for his desk, as a pencil holder. I felt it represented his brand, it looked beautiful and was actually useful. It's not too big so he won't put it away in a box or drawer and forget about it, so therefore he will enjoy that gift and in return he will keep me in mind more often, he will remember who gave it to him and make a connection. It's a simple idea but one that works for both parties and comes from a sincere place.

• • •

Another way I practised attention to detail and building my own personal brand in my Formula 1 career was with sponsors. Much as I'd love to just drive cars, earn a lot of money and go home, I realised very quickly that racing was only one part of the job. In F1, sponsors are the lifeblood of the sport in many ways, their funding can be the difference between a team doing well or not existing at all. They are, after all, the customers of the team, the companies to which the team has sold marketing services. It's not just about the money, to be fair. F1 sponsors are lauded primarily for the finance they bring but some of them may be technology sponsors as well, such as a company that offers computing, software, or technology packages that facilitate what the team needs to do next to improve.

You might think the whole sponsor world in F1 is too corporate, too self-indulgent; in the football world it's certainly been heavily criticised as a culture, with all the talk of 'prawn sandwiches' taking the game away from the 'real' fans. In Formula 1, however, without sponsors there would not be as many teams, that's just a fact. Therefore, necessarily, as a driver, part of your role is to keep sponsors happy, that goes with the territory and I never had a problem with that. My approach to these events is to see them as just another opportunity to pay attention to detail, and simply represents an extension of what my father always said: be smart, be on time, present yourself well.

It is not enough to simply put a company's logo on the driver's helmet or car. The sponsors are no longer satisfied with just getting publicity at 20 Formula 1 races around the world; instead they expect a 365-day marketing programme that covers a wide range of activities and goals they have set for us to achieve. It used to be that big sponsors came into Formula 1 hoping that they would benefit from the television coverage generated by winning races and seeing their brands on TV. However, no team in Formula 1 can guarantee that they will win every race. A team like McLaren has a fantastic record, but ultimately their achievement of winning 25 per cent of all the Formula 1 races in which they have competed since the 1960s means that 75 per cent of the time their sponsors are going to be disappointed if the only thing that matters is winning on TV.

Sponsors expect – and deserve – a good return on their investment in a number of ways. So as well as visibility and attendance at actual races, they will also expect to benefit from a wide range of marketing activities and events. A typical function would be meeting ten or so high net-worth individuals from a bank for dinner where you shine a light on F1, a different business and industry from theirs. People are curious to know what Formula 1 is like, so that becomes a conversation point for then moving their business forward. Sports is very universal, it offers an escape from reality and has an amazing ability to bring people together from all walks of life. I enjoyed meeting all these different people, some were hugely successful, others weren't, but I could learn from most of them.

Some drivers don't enjoy the feeling of being 'paraded' but I never had a problem with that. Each to their own, of course. Jacques Villeneuve, who is a friend, a brilliant driver and a great guy, had all sorts of clauses in his contract to predetermine that an appearance would be only so long, it would maybe be at his hotel. At times I'm sure that was just painful from a team point of view. He didn't particularly want to do those events, and he certainly wasn't alone in that in the pit lane. He was also always a bit more grungy, which to be fair was of his time and of his age. He always used to take the mickey out of me slightly by saying I was 'always dressed smartly and smiling and saying yes', but today I would suggest that he now understands and recognises why I did that. Quite a few drivers take the view of 'That's not my job. I'm being paid to be a racing driver, is it really my job to smile with the media, is it really my job to do a sponsor dinner and talk to other people?' Well, actually, in my opinion, yes it is. That's what I was being paid for, to be a public face of the team and a representative of the company, and therefore I was happy to do everything that was asked of me and do it to the best of my ability.

Besides, some of these sponsor events were fantastic fun! I've done a parabolic flight at zero gravity; I went to Star City in Moscow and ran loads of tests with astronauts; I have been to mud spas in Slovakia and been rubbed up in front of the media; I've done doughnuts on the heliport on top of Dubai's 7-star Burj Al Arab hotel in a Formula 1 car; I've raced an F1 car through various cities of the world in front of thousands of people; I've driven through Petra in an F1 car... how can any of these 'obligations' be a bad thing? I always looked at the sponsor obligations like this: firstly, it's my contracted job; secondly, as I just said, some of these events are amazing, it's a privileged position to be in; thirdly, it's also part of my responsibility to make these events engaging and fun so that people buy into it, the sponsors, the fans, the media enjoy themselves, and everyone is happy to be there.

For teams like McLaren, Red Bull and Williams, part of my role as a driver is that we are working to add value to our sponsors/customers all year round, seven days a week, and the racing becomes only one part of what we do for them. As a driver, I am the external face of the team and often the person who all our sponsors (or the media or fans) want to meet. So a key part of my job – that needs paying attention to – is to present the best possible image of the team and their core values. I viewed myself as an ambassador of the company and obliged to do a lot more than just think about my job driving the car. This didn't just apply at official events – as somebody who is perceived to have a public profile to some degree, I was acutely aware of how my behaviour might impact on people I work with. Like I just said, I felt that I represented all the people I worked with and if I do something in the public eye which is embarrassing, such as falling drunk out of a nightclub, then I am letting those people down. Not every driver sees it that way, but that's just my view. (The images online of me falling over drunk outside a nightclub are clearly photoshopped!)

Consequently, I have spent my career working with brands that use F1 as a platform for their positioning and promotion, with me as one of the assets. Since I retired, some of my most important work has been as a brand ambassador – and I have had to develop my own 'brand strategy' accordingly. As a result, even though I no longer race around Grands Prix, I continue to be a brand ambassador and do promotional and marketing events all over the world for a range of companies who want to be associated with me, such as Mercedes, Red Bull, IWC Watches, Heineken, UBS, Cooper Tires, Transcal and Hugo Boss. With this in mind, I am aware that I represent my own brand, and that is something that Sir Jackie Stewart instilled in me from the moment he phoned me up in my dad's garage.

Besides, I believe I learnt so much from interacting with all these sponsors. Very often they were incredibly successful individuals who were fascinating to be around and would offer many pearls of wisdom, if you were motivated enough to listen. I feel lucky that I was able to learn the art of the cocktail party and also observe how these huge companies work, which has been immensely useful since retiring. Had I not paid attention to the detail of these events and made a real effort to engage in them, I doubt very much whether I would have had the skills and the contacts to be in that same position today.

• • •

You might ask, 'What is the benefit of all this attention to detail? Is it not just excessively particular?' Not at all. There is a very real and tangible benefit regardless of whether you are in sport, business, self-employed, an employee, whatever your circumstance: the customer, client, sponsor, boss all benefit from your exacting attention to detail.

Let's look at hotels. When I was a partner in The Columbus Hotel in Monaco, I wanted to pay attention to the small detail so that guests always felt that every single aspect of their stay had been covered and considered. For example, it certainly wasn't unheard of for me to clean the toilets in the common areas if I found them less than acceptable. However, there are plenty of people who would say, 'I'm not doing that because it's not my job and that's below my perceived position in life'. Don't get me wrong, I'd rather not clean the toilets when I'm in Monaco, but my attitude was always, 'Right, I don't really want to do this but it needs doing so let's get stuck in and get it done well.' You probably didn't think you'd get a anecdote about cleaning a toilet from a business book but that was always just something that I couldn't leave unattended. Related to that, never think that you are above a certain task. A lot of successful business people start taking the view of 'That's not my job'. They'll walk past some litter on the floor because they think they are above picking it up; 'Let the cleaner get that.' Really? That is not acceptable behaviour.

Getting back to attention to detail, another example would be how, as I get older, my eyesight isn't as sharp as it once was. That's just natural. So why do I get in some hotel showers and there's bottles of shampoo and conditioner with tiny writing on them? I can't tell which is which. The bottle is big enough to carry larger lettering, but someone hasn't thought about that. They've designed a free bottle of shampoo to look expensive and sleek, but one that many people won't be able to read. That might not bother you at all, but it's just a small example of thinking through every detail of your business with the customer in mind. I don't think people think the detail through as well as they should, sometimes. If you own a hotel, walk to a room from the concierge, go into the room, imagine you are checking in: what do you want to see? Have you really thought through *every* detail? It's all in the detail.

· · ·

Paying precise attention to detail is something that F1 excels at. Like your business or career, every great team in F1 needs to be aware that unless they have paid complete attention to detail, they will not be able to produce the best possible outcome. In Formula 1 we like to come up with a comprehensive solution for what we want to achieve, rather than focusing on one element; in other words, attention is paid to *every detail*, not just one aspect. The best analogy of our approach to paying meticulous attention to detail is in the Formula 1 car itself.

An F1 car is made up of more than 5,000 individual components, and within these we have significant systems or structures that have to perform very highly and also work together in harmony. You have the chassis, which is made from carbon fibre and has a number of jobs to do; it has to first of all provide somewhere for me to sit, which is quite useful, be physically large enough for me to operate all the systems, yet small enough to make the car aerodynamically efficient. It also has to have the strength to protect me in the event of a 200mph accident, perhaps with multiple impacts, and be stiff and strong enough to carry all of the other components of the car that are bolted to it.

Then you have the engine, which these days not only produces almost 1000bhp and powers the car around the track, but is itself part of the chassis, so it has to be rigid, as well as reliable and fuel-efficient. The gearbox comes next, transferring the power to the wheels, and then you have the suspension on all four corners, and finally the bodywork, including the front and rear wings, the floor section and all the other efficiently designed pieces of carbon fibre which enable the car to produce over two tonnes of downforce at top speed. (Quick aside: the urban myth is true, an F1 car could quite literally drive upside down as the downforce generated is more than double the weight of the car and driver combined.)

We call this assembly of all these elements, all these independently designed systems which go into making a car, the 'package'. The best 'package' is what we are looking for and a good package is a car that has all of these systems working in harmony, complementing each other and enabling me as a driver to take performance on to a new level. A great package has had painstaking attention paid to every single component so that they integrate as well as possible.

As you will recall, at our factories we have hundreds of skilled people responsible for the design and manufacture of the different systems – the 85 per cent of our staff who do not actually travel to races – all paying focused attention to their challenges: experts in structural design, vehicle dynamics, aerodynamics, power train design, electronics, software and control systems. Although each of these people might like to come up with simply the best in their respective area, the fact is we have to develop a complete solution that works together for the benefit of me, the driver, as the end user. Each one of those people is applying intense attention to detail so that every part and sub-assembly within the car is exactly as it should be. It is a company culture that has to be adopted by absolutely everyone. One weak link could lead to a parts failure that could be disastrous.

You can't win races by producing only the best engine or gearbox. F1 teams have to be focused on packaging the best overall solution and ultimately that's what the championship-winning teams are able to do. At McLaren, we won the team's championship in 1998 because we produced the best overall car solution over the course of the season. We did that by paying attention to every tiny detail.

Do you or your company pay attention to the tiny detail? Do you really prepare as you should? *Really?* Are you therefore able to offer a comprehensive solution to your customers? Never, ever forget the detail.

CHAPTER 7
INNOVATING TO WIN

You may apply many of the ideas we've already talked about in this book but come up against someone who has taken an identical approach. However, one area where you can offer yourself the best chance of beating your competitors is when you innovate.

Formula 1, arguably more than any other sport, is absolutely fantastic at doing exactly that. Genuine innovation is the very oxygen on which the sport thrives. I was around innovative thinking on an almost daily basis for all of my racing career. Being in F1 means you are surrounded by people who try to think differently. F1 has had to adapt many times, in fact, I would say that rapid innovation is the defining characteristic of the sport. By contrast, so many businesses are stuck in their ways, still very profitable and successful, which is great, but that success breeds a degree of complacency and ultimately that will degrade the power of the team and company. There is a quote often attributed to Bill Gates, who knows a wee thing about business I think it's fair to say: 'Success is a lousy teacher. It seduces smart people into thinking they can't lose.' I quite like that. I see it so often at senior levels within big business. Something that success can lead you to forget about is innovation and its close bedfellow, transformation.

I'd like to take this opportunity to detail at length various innovations from these teams that I was involved with that are superb examples of the thinking needed to innovate but also the enormous performance benefits that await those who are brave enough to go for it. First up, McLaren. Historically, that team has always been about innovation, doing things differently from the competition and being prepared to experiment and take the odd risk. A significant example would be when they became the first team to manufacture a Formula 1 car using carbon fibre – universal now, but at the time that was a giant leap forward. Composite materials had been around for some time, and a fully composite-bodied car was even prototyped by scientists back in the late 1940s. By the 1960s, Britain was pioneering the tech but it wasn't until 1981 when the geniuses at McLaren saw the benefits to motorsport of an incredibly strong material that was also extremely lightweight. In that year they launched the first ever carbon-fibre monocoque, masterminded by designer John Barnard. Despite F1's history of innovation, many established teams were very doubtful that this new material would work, with many fearing that this 'black plastic' might just disappear into clouds of dust in a big crash.

However, McLaren believed in their innovation and committed to introducing it in competitive racing, launching the pioneering MP4/1 in March of that year. The car was driven by John Watson to victory at the British Grand Prix but it was actually a ferocious accident at Monza that illustrated the extent of McLaren's foresight. Due to the severity of the crash, most witnesses assumed Watson was dead; in fact, he emerged unscathed. In an instant, conventional chassis construction was obsolete. What followed was a mad rush by the other teams to replicate the McLaren innovation, but of course Ron Dennis and John Barnard had stolen a march on their rivals by pursuing innovation, transforming the way an F1 car is constructed and having the courage of their convictions.

Another major innovation from that highly inventive team could be found on the McLaren-Mercedes MP4/12 of 1997 and its successor, the MP4/13 of 1998. This came in the form of having a fourth pedal in the cockpit, alongside the standard brake, throttle and clutch set-up. This additional pedal could be set up to provide braking to either the left or right rear brake, and later to switch between both, which would have the effect of helping the car to use the brakes to steer it more efficiently through a corner. The concept is similar to what you would see on a tracked vehicle, such as a military tank or on earth-moving equipment; if you stop the right-hand track, the vehicle will turn right, if you stop the left-hand track, the opposite will happen.

It was McLaren's American design engineer Steve Nichols who came up with the idea during the winter of 1996/97 and coaxed the team, under chief designer Neil Oatley, into trying it out at the end of a test day in the spring. The actual mechanics of making it work were simplicity itself, requiring a second brake pedal to be added, a T-type connector on the primary brake master cylinder and an additional master cylinder on the brake line feeding the inside rear wheel. In essence, it was a plumbing job!

The effect was immediate, and was estimated by the team to be worth as much as 0.5–0.7s per lap on an average Formula 1 circuit. It was particularly effective on circuits with a proliferation of 90-degree 'stop–go' corners where understeer could be an issue. It was also a great way to ensure that the car could cope with a more aerodynamically beneficial understeer-promoting set-up. Unfortunately, the McLaren team's 1997 season was marred by poor reliability, with 14 car retirements in 17 races. After one of those failures, at the Luxembourg Grand Prix at the Nürburgring, Darren Heath, one of Formula 1's leading photographers, had the presence of mind to lean into the cockpit of Mika Häkkinen's car and shoot off a series of photographs of the footwell. He had become suspicious there was something going on because, while taking photographs trackside, he noticed that our rear inside brake disks were red-hot mid-corner! These photographs were published, causing something of a sensation, as they proved conclusively what many suspected: McLaren had a secret braking system.

As with the carbon-fibre monocoque, other teams immediately tried to copy what they believed McLaren to be doing but, as ever with innovations, just copying what you see is seldom going to work. This is where 'first mover advantage' came into play for McLaren as they had long realised that there was a little more to making it work than the original plumbing solution had suggested. Managing brake temperatures as well as running a specific type of brake material were all part of the overall requirement, and they had spent many months refining the overall system.

Suffice to say that no one else made it work, and when McLaren turned up at the first round of the 1998 World Championship with the new Adrian Newey-designed McLaren MP4/13, the competition was given an object lesson in domination. Having been up to two seconds per lap faster than the competition in pre-season testing, Mika and I dominated qualifying with our brake-steering cars, almost a full second faster than our nearest rival, and then proceeded to do the same in the race.

Mika slightly overheated his rear brake, such was his enthusiasm for the system, and this caused some concern within the team, leading to a confused radio communication that resulted in him making an unnecessary pit stop; fortunately, this handed the lead to me, but I later allowed Häkkinen to retake the lead once the team had explained the mistake to me over the radio. We duly took a perfect 1–2 finish.

Immediately after this race, the unique brake steering was declared illegal, even though it had been in operation for almost a full year, and was immediately consigned to the history books. Despite this premature end to a very clever system, it remains a very good example of innovation catching rivals out almost without reply.

If companies such as McLaren are perfect examples of innovators within F1, then Adrian Newey is a great personal example – we can all learn so much from his ability to look at completely new ideas that no one else seems to have considered. He is somehow able to look at a car that the entire paddock is analysing, and yet dream up a new solution to changed regulations or tighter restrictions that no one else has thought of.

One element of this characteristic is the way he is so good at encouraging debate, something that stimulates great innovation. With his reputation and presence in a room, it would be easy for people to shy away from voicing an opinion. It would also be very easy for Adrian to walk in, tell people his idea and then steamroller that through. In actual fact, Adrian's approach seems to allow his team to challenge him when they feel they have a good idea. If they can prove they are right, then he has no problem adopting that design or approach. Innovation is proactively encouraged. If you think about it, if an idea is truly innovative, then there is every chance that when you first hear of the notion, you might think it is not going to work. Adrian never has a closed mind and the consequence of that attitude is plain for all to see.

Adrian also has this innate ability to think differently from his competitors. The cliché is 'think outside the box', and Adrian certainly does that. There are numerous examples within F1 of him completely stealing a march over his rivals with brilliant ideas. Extremely tight packaging of car bodywork for aerodynamic reasons was first seen on his March designs of late 1980s. Adrian developed a significant aerodynamic innovation on the Leyton House March 881 Formula 1 cars of 1988. They raised the front nose, creating the high nose, which has been a feature of F1 car designs ever since. With that design came the single-piece front wing, thus replacing the two-piece units that used to be separated by the nose cone. This promoted a much more efficient front wing, and the raised nose also allowed great airflow management to the underside of the car. It can thus be said that the 881 was a ground-breaking car that influenced F1 car design for the next 30 years. *That* is the level of innovation that someone like Adrian can operate at.

However, to illustrate this chapter's theme in more depth, I'd like to focus on Adrian's Williams FW17B in which I scored my first Grand Prix victory in Portugal in 1995. It is my favourite Formula 1 car I have raced. The FW17B is also a very fine illustration of the kind of innovation for which Adrian Newey has become famous.

This, in turn, is a great example to show how innovation needs to be comprehensive, offer a holistic solution and, if necessary, use non-conventional ideas. The innovation and developments that made the FW17 noteworthy stem from the fact that it was born out of Adrian's deep understanding of the problems that afflicted its predecessor, the FW16, the car in which Ayrton Senna lost his life at the 1994 San Marino Grand Prix. So clearly this particular innovation was incredibly pertinent to myself.

The problems that afflicted the Williams-Renault FW16 had their origins in a huge change in the technical regulations prior to the 1994 season. Active suspension systems, and a host of other electronic aids, which Williams had been able to use to good effect in winning both the 1993 World Championships, were suddenly outlawed. External regulation stifling innovation is nothing new in Formula 1, as in many industries, and this particular change put the Williams team behind the competition.

Compromised by this change, the FW16 was also afflicted with a degree of aerodynamic instability, which plagued Ayrton Senna and Damon Hill in the opening two races of the 1994 season. This led to Adrian carrying out detailed investigations which, he admitted in his 2017 book *How to Build a Car*, led to a 'eureka' moment when he found that the car's lengthy side pods were causing an aerodynamic imbalance known as flow separation. Senna's death at the third round of the World Championship was not in itself caused by that instability issue, but in the wake of that tragedy Newey's determination to rid the car of its aerodynamic problems led to a significant mid-season upgrade.

These upgrades ultimately influenced and benefited the following season's FW17, including shortening the side pods and raising the nose of the car to create a much cleaner airflow to the underbody, including the all-important floor section and rear diffuser. The driver's seating position was also revised, resulting in the front suspension being relocated and the steering column being raised. The progress made with the aerodynamics on the original FW17 led to a further, mid-season development with the introduction of a much-improved rear diffuser and a revised car designated the FW17B.

The Williams-Renault FW17B was introduced in time for the 1995 Portuguese Grand Prix, and I managed to claim both pole position and an admittedly dominant race victory, finishing more than seven seconds ahead of Michael Schumacher's Benetton, with the second Williams of teammate Damon Hill 22 seconds back in third place. Starting with the fundamental problems that had compromised the FW16 of 18 months previously, the FW17B demonstrated Adrian's inherent ability to get on top of a problem and then to drive change and evolution, refining the solution until it achieves its targets. A great example of Formula 1-style constant innovation and development.

The FW17B is also an example of how, when you think about innovation, there is often a tendency to look for the big idea, the ground-breaking change that disrupts an entire industry, when in fact we often see that by fully understanding the things that have not worked well in the past, we can drive brilliant – or at least better – solutions.

Finally, in terms of Adrian's innovation, it's worth pointing out how artistic his work is – progress need not be ugly and functional. Take the new Aston Martin Valkyrie hypercar, designed in collaboration with Red Bull Technologies. I think it's a beautiful looking car, essentially a real-life example of being inside Adrian's mind. That's what he sees as design in terms of looking good as opposed to just being functional. And yet he is somehow able to be this innovative while all the time mixing his engineering brilliance with art. If Adrian has a choice between something that looks good and delivers, versus something that doesn't look good but might have more potential, he'll go for the first option. His designs usually look beautiful; where something may have functionality but doesn't look good, he will try and find another route. Other designers might just go, 'Well, look, it's got functionality, it works, let's do it and move on.' The problem is that way you eventually end up with one big lump of functionality and ugliness. They do say a winning car looks beautiful. So even Adrian's approach to innovation is unconventional – and let's face it, his record speaks for itself. Ten World Championship

titles across three teams. That's what can happen when you innovate
and question established thinking.

. . .

Even if you are not the individual who has personally innovated and
considered how things might be done differently, there is no excuse
for you not to adopt and champion new ways of thinking. Your
personal and company culture should look to adopt new, innovative
technology. If you don't, your competitors will. In F1 it is a given
that all teams are relentlessly searching for the next technological
advance and if you fall off the pace in that area then you sure as
hell will fall off the pace on track if something significant comes
along. There's really no excuse. Many years ago, when information
technology was relatively new to the sport, there was a generation of
old-school engineers who were sometimes reluctant to work with
the 'new-fangled' bits of kit; there was also a very real risk of the
embryonic technology failing or not doing its job very well. That's
all a thing of the past now and yet I still meet people in business who
seem wary of new technology, who are slow or reluctant to adopt
new systems and technologies.

I would never have been able to last in F1 if that had been
my approach. My career has been made all the more fascinating
because it coincided perfectly with the information technology
revolution arriving in Formula 1. When I started in F1 as test
driver for the Williams team, testing and development had only

recently evolved from the era of hand-written notes, clipboards and designs based on human experience – and sometimes a 'hunch' or 'educated guesswork'.

As I've detailed, I started by working with former World Champions Alain Prost and Ayrton Senna. What systems we had – with laptops plugged into the cars whenever we stopped in order to download some basic information – were state-of-the-art at the time, but I now realise how agricultural everything was; the systems and even the cars themselves. Yes, we had innovation but the most we could hope for was three or perhaps four upgrades to the car during the racing season. A lot of the time we were stuck with the car – and any problems – for race after race.

F1 innovation is now so frantic and fast-paced that teams expect to bring new developments or upgrades to each race, sometimes only one week apart, and anywhere in the world. Over the last 20 years the advent of 3D CAD modelling, CFD (computational fluid dynamics) and rapid prototyping including 3D printing means that we can ask for new aerodynamic components or a software change which might eradicate a bug in the system from one race to the next.

As a result of the teams having access to smart, interconnected and innovative technology, we are able to work together in ways that, not so long ago, could only be dreamt of. When I was growing up in Scotland in the 1970s, for example, a great driver such as Jackie could easily suffer a failure in the race due to a small problem that no one knew anything about, and even if they did they couldn't fix it during the race anyway.

Thanks to people and technology working together, my experience was rather different. I can offer several examples where technology was of huge benefit to my race. For instance, it was in part data that enabled me to win the 2002 Monaco Grand Prix – my second victory around the street of the principality where I reside. Starting from second place on the grid, I made a great start and was able to take the lead away from pole-man Juan Pablo Montoya, who later fell into the clutches of Michael Schumacher. Schumacher and myself then battled for the rest of the race, seldom separated by more than one second. At that point, no one on my team – including myself – realised that I had started to develop a potentially significant problem with my car. Fortunately, thanks to the fast-developing field of telematics and data analysis that was sweeping through F1, my team was able to pinpoint the problem and create a solution.

The issue was spotted thanks to the real-time data being analysed by our technicians sitting in front of computer racks. The problem was a faulty solenoid on the oil system, which was allowing a secondary oil tank known as a 'top-up tank' to overfill, spilling oil into the air intake and causing the engine to burn excess oil in addition to race fuel. Debris was the likely cause of the fault, but the team could see on its telemetry system the relevant data from the engine and oil system sensors. After some analysis, the team deployed a solution by activating the system fully with the intention of clearing any debris and allowing the system to reset. The solution worked perfectly, the issue was eliminated in my car and after that I was able to hold Schumacher at bay, eventually winning the race by 1.05 seconds. Without the team's use of innovative technology and precise data and their fast, incisive reaction to what it was telling them, that could not have happened. Innovation, teamwork, performance and risk management, all in one afternoon.

So you absolutely must immerse yourself in innovation and the new technologies affecting your career or business. You don't always need to spot problems yourself to fuel this impetus – sometimes it will be feedback off customers or staff within the business that drive key new ideas.

Here is a very feedback-driven innovation within F1 that I am proud to have been very involved with: the head and neck support device, or HANS as we call it. This was developed after Senna's fatal accident, and I remember Doctor Robert Hubbard from Michigan State University bringing the prototype to F1 where it was immediately championed by the senior medical expert, Professor Sid Watkins. The concept was to create a U-shaped carbon frame that slipped over the driver's shoulders and behind the neck, then attached to the helmet; the idea was to reduce head and neck trauma by decelerating the head in a controlled way during a high-speed accident.

The problem was that the early ones were uncomfortable – clearly, even with such honourable intentions, if a new device makes driving these hugely challenging machines even more tricky, then it could easily be self-defeating. It had to be fit for purpose and to everyone's credit they did not just design a theoretical HANS device and then issue that, they actively sought out feedback from drivers.

I was one of the drivers approached and so I worked with the then-President of the FIA, Max Mosley, to fast-track a revised seat belt design fitted with a second adjuster so that the HANS device slipped between a second strap and wasn't resting against the driver's body, which was uncomfortable. I gave them feedback that no crash test dummy ever could, and that made all the difference: this was about safety but also ergonomics and making sure that the final solution was not only effective but practical. I am very proud of helping in some small way and I take my hat off to the FIA for seeking that feedback and responding to it.

Of course, innovation and technology is not a one-way street of exclusive benefits and zero risk. The speed of modern life is now so fast that it can be a minefield in terms of individuals in sport and business using technology, specifically social media – an innovation that nearly everyone seems to have adopted. As a commentator, I now have to consider that our programming is being watched live or relayed on TV and followed on the website, being saved and replayed on smartphones and tablets on catch-up TV, and being discussed, often in real-time, across social networks such as Twitter, Instagram and Facebook.

For the majority of my career as a Formula 1 driver, all my communication with the media and the general public was channeled and controlled through my team's press department, so there was no risk of me saying anything out of turn! That's all changed now that all the drivers have their personal Twitter, Instagram and Facebook accounts, which enable them to interact with the public, including the media, faster than their teams can keep up. Some of this can be very entertaining, but there is also a serious dimension to it such as when Lewis Hamilton caused a stir at the Belgian Grand Prix by tweeting a screen-shot of his McLaren's qualifying data to show everyone the difference in performance between his car and that of teammate Jenson Button. If data is the key to helping a team to achieve success within Formula 1, the reverse can also be true. Data security is a legitimate concern for all businesses, and Formula 1 is no different. Lewis's small misdemeanour could have had potentially serious implications for his team.

Further, innovation for the sake of it is not necessarily a benefit and, worse still, innovation that proves impractical is merely a waste of time, energy and money. So if you are thinking of introducing new tech into your business, make sure it is real-time tested; don't let some mega-geek design a new system that has never been test-driven by the people who are going to use it every day. Theory and practice have to be married together otherwise innovation achieves very little.

Once again it was my steering wheel that gave rise to an example of the way things can develop. From a driver's point of view, of course, a key aspect of design is ergonomics because I want to be comfortable, safe and secure in the cockpit as well as be able to reach all the necessary controls, which these days are quite complex. This is particularly true of the steering wheel, which has a range of systems for the driver to operate; this includes the quickshift gearbox actuators on the rear of the steering wheel, a hand clutch and more than 40 buttons, dials and toggles.

In a two-car Formula 1 team, the best layout for the steering wheel is one that is common to both drivers, and a key factor in this is whether you are right- or left-handed. If there is a clear number-one driver in a team, he might have first choice on the steering wheel layout, but when I worked with Mika Häkkinen at McLaren, for example, we put our individual requirements forward to the team.

The wheel design has to be fit for purpose because I want my design engineers to understand that the wheel is constantly moving, that the car is bouncing over the kerbs and bumps, and that whatever is happening I need to be able to access the right systems in the most efficient way possible. For example, when you are driving an F1 car and gripping the steering wheel in both hands, you want to be able to use your thumb to adjust the most frequently used systems at 160mph in a 5g corner. It's important that the design engineers understand that everything is not happening in a straight line and in a calm moment, and that taking your hand off the steering wheel at these speeds is not ideal!

I think it's really important that the designers put themselves in the position of their 'customer', the driver – and go outside the comfort of the design office. To create useable innovation. Let me give you another example. There was a new designer at McLaren who was making the pedals smaller and lighter and therefore saving weight. He completed his design and was able to tick his own personal box of delivering a better package and lighter pedal box. However, I took the pedals out on track and it was not good at all. What he didn't know – because he hadn't spoken to me, the driver – was that the pedal still needed to be a certain mass (especially the brake) because of the extreme load that we press through that pedal. So I went to meet him to talk this through and I asked him to call up the drawings of these new lighter pedals on the CAD system. Then, as he was doing that, I shook the back of his office chair violently and, of course, he struggled to control the mouse. He looked at me bemused and I said, 'That is my office, it shakes, it's violent, it's noisy, it's hard to focus, that's where I have to use these pedals.' He had designed a beautiful pedal box in a totally sterile environment that was intended for use in an incredibly aggressive and hostile environment. You've got to know your customer, and how they will use your product, before you innovate.

It is for this reason that these days some F1 design offices will have a complete car in the middle of the room, so that the designers can physically check the outcome of what they are doing and understand its effect on the drivers or even the engineers and mechanics who have to work on the cars in a demanding environment. Does your business have that level of focus on innovation being seamlessly useable?

If you are the leader or owner of a company, then it is your direct responsibility to encourage innovation and a culture of creativity. You do that by making everyone believe that their ideas will be listened to. It's down to leadership. People need to feel they can question an idea or strategy, or that they can propose an idea that might sound unorthodox at first. You can't innovate alone. You need to generate an atmosphere where people – whether that is seasoned colleagues or young guns just starting out – feel able to speak up. If the CEO is not to be challenged or is the only one who can put ideas forward, then how is that going to encourage creativity? It's about empowering people, that is how you encourage creativity.

Recognising that driving an innovation culture is not always plain sailing, you need to be immersed in it at least in a way that equips your business with a keen hunger for new ideas. Ask yourself honestly: do you ask questions internally in your company about how technology and innovation could improve the set-up? Are you aware of issues in areas where you are not involved on a daily basis that might benefit from a fresh pair of eyes or new ideas? Do you ever instigate a programme of analysis and then support genuine innovation to discover new solutions? Do you really, genuinely, think outside of the box?

CHAPTER 8
EFFICIENCY, EXECUTION AND CUSTOMER SERVICE

Don't some people send ridiculously long emails? And what do you do when they send you a two- or three-page email? I bet you don't read it all, do you? Certainly not in any depth, anyway. Classic inefficiency.

Formula 1 doesn't tolerate inefficiency and neither should you. I'm a great believer in the idea that you've only got so much energy each day, nobody has infinite energy, so to be successful you need to deploy that energy in efficient ways and focus it on elements that are genuinely important.

One of the most important ways to be efficient is to strive for productive use of your time. Sounds simple, but so many company cultures let this slip. A Formula 1 racing driver can't afford to be unproductive because most elite-level sport is very rarely a long-lasting career over many decades. We essentially live the life of a mayfly: we are born, eat, reproduce, die, all in a very short window of time. I'm not sure that's how most Formula 1 experts would describe the potential career of a racing driver, but it's a fact that us racing drivers absolutely compress our role into a much shorter period than so-called 'normal' careers. There is a hugely beneficial consequence of living life as a mayfly: you learn to value every day, every hour, even every second. If you meet with an ex-Formula 1 racer, you will notice that, in the majority, their perception of time is finely tuned into every second of every day. They hate being unproductive and are always looking to maximise what tasks can get done each day. Again, efficiency.

Are you truly productive each day? Do you enjoy completing tasks? I'm at my best when I'm busy. During those times, if someone asks me to do something I try to do it straight away. This is largely because writing something down to remind me to do a task later often takes almost as much time as just doing the request then and there. Of course, there are times when you are just jumping on a plane or you can't take a phone call, but if you are in the office being busy, then if a request comes in, if it's quick or just needs a swift email, do it straight away. Otherwise, it will just clutter your inbox and also your mind and lie there in waiting till you do it anyway. That's being inefficient.

This is a skill that you learn over time – I think my parents helped me, they were very much of the mind to 'Get up, get on, get the job done, move on to the next thing'. I find it incredible to see how many people, even at the upper levels of business, tend to postpone till tomorrow, tomorrow, tomorrow. There are a lot of things that we don't like to do but we've just got to do it. Just get on and do it.

This brings me on to the subject of deadlines. Someone once said the truth, 'Nothing ever gets done without a deadline'. Yet, so many people sail past deadlines so nonchalantly that you wonder if they ever had any intention of meeting the target date in the first place. When I see product launches slip a day or a week, I often think, *That would just not work in F1*. My sport works to absolute deadlines. A Formula 1 race is a completely immoveable deadline and one of the ultimate exercises in efficiency. For example, the red lights go out at two o'clock in Melbourne on the third weekend of March. Fact. That cannot change. The race goes on with or without you. A Grand Prix *will* start on time – with 20 cars, ten teams, 60 technical staff per team, 20 marketing, catering, PR and management staff, making 80 team personnel at each race; add to that the 200 officials, 300 track workers, 800 media of all kinds including production teams and you are heading into the region of 2,500 people working at each Grand Prix, watched by around 100 million people live on TV – no pressure! They all manage to get to Melbourne at that time and be ready at precisely the moment the red light goes out. No ifs or buts, no excuses. By going racing all around the world every two weeks, Formula 1 proves that by setting hard deadlines and having the right efficient principles in place, then punctual delivery can be achieved time after time if you really want to. So it can be done.

People make all sorts of excuses for being late, and sometimes they are even feasible but, again, in F1 there can be no such justification. Imagine if Red Bull was absent from the grid and they said it was because they'd 'got behind schedule, sorry'. Or what if they said, 'Sorry, we've had a few issues, we will be on the grid at twenty past'!

Formula 1's efficiency is even more impressive when you consider the scale of the annual challenge facing the teams: remember, the goalposts are almost constantly changing – each year our sports governing body, the FIA, changes the rules and regulations in an effort to slow the cars down and make sure we are as safe as possible. Simultaneously, inside the team we aim to innovate, extract additional performance and find a competitive advantage over our competition. Each team has a little over six months to design and manufacture a brand-new Formula 1 car ahead of the season. This means that all 800 to 900 staff must be fully aligned behind the project plan and the deadlines which everyone has set. We have to pass all the regulatory checks by a certain date, take part in pre-season testing on a given day, and then turn up at precisely the right time for 20 Grands Prix all around the world, from March through to November. When you think of the ultra-complex operation that running an F1 team represents, if they can do it why can't all businesses?

It's a simple matter of efficiency and execution. As a consequence of this quite brilliant culture in the paddock, you meet all sorts of people in F1 who are staggeringly efficient. Here's a few examples to think about and hopefully be inspired by. First up, Sir Patrick Head, the original partner of Sir Frank Williams at the team. During my time at Williams, I worked closely with Patrick and he was a very strong and impressive character. Regarded as one of the leading engineers and technical directors in Formula 1 for over 30 years, Patrick started his professional life in the Royal Navy before graduating with a degree in mechanical engineering from UCL. His early motor-racing career was spent working for Lola in Huntingdon, Cambridge, but it was the partnership forged with Frank Williams in 1977 that spawned one of Formula 1's greatest success stories. With Frank looking after the commercial side of the business, Patrick oversaw the technical operations, jointly leading to nine World Championships for Constructors and seven World Championships for Drivers.

Patrick is famous for taking a no-nonsense approach to racing, and for those on the receiving end of his booming voice, life could sometimes appear unforgiving. He remains, enormously popular within the sport, and is responsible for helping to mentor and launch the careers of top designers including Adrian Newey, Ross Brawn, Rory Byrne, Neil Oatley and Frank Dernie.

Like Adrian Newey, Patrick has this very precise ability to zone in on any given problem. As a driver, you will go on track and test a car for him, then come back in and he will simply say, 'What is the biggest problem, DC? Tell us what you need. What do we need to do?' Very short questions. No waffle. Very energy-efficient. The opposite of the person that we all know who says, 'I'm so busy, busy, busy', while they lean up against a wall making small talk for 20 minutes without pausing for breath. Saying you're busy when you're not just doesn't cut it in a world full of busy people. Patrick uses five words where others would use 50, and he still gets to the exact root of the problem.

Another phenomenally efficient person I came across in motor racing was Alain Prost. In fact, his nickname The Professor was partly due to his very efficient way of analysing challenges and working with the car and team. For example, he had an acute ability to manage fuel loads, tyres and other technical elements of the car because of his inherent mechanical sympathy, and therefore complete a race when so many other drivers around him were unable to get their car to the finish line. In my experience, Prost didn't actually do a lot of laps in testing, but when he did do them he was always very efficient. *Every single lap counted.* Every single run offered some tiny piece of information that he was very articulate at relating back to the team so that they were able to learn from that, as he was. He viewed every lap as a learning curve. I learnt that from him: don't do laps for the sake of it. Testing has to be as important as racing. You may not have the chequered flag at the end and win race points or a podium, but you still have to approach testing in the same way. Likewise, in business, every event has to be tackled like it is the biggest and best event you've ever done. That is something I learnt from Prost.

Seb Vettel is an incredibly efficient driver. He uses his time very precisely, there is very little, if any, wastage. He doesn't do social media and many of the extra-curricular things that drivers such as Lewis do. Does that affect his income stream? Yes. Some people consider his 'brand' is diminished because he can be perceived as inaccessible and slightly remote. Does that affect his life negatively? Not in his opinion; he chooses to live a different way. However, that has no reflection on his approach in the factory or on track. It's certainly more efficient in terms of freeing up time to work on the car or with the team. He is a great example of a driver who, like the champions and great drivers before him, has a commitment to the debrief and the detail, is incredibly efficient at focusing on what is needed. Seb is also very good at looking the person in the eye who can deliver what he needs and making them feel that it's not just any old job for them to deliver. They are part of an emotional process. That in turn makes them far more efficient, so he is able to refine the whole process throughout the team.

Another very efficient figure I've worked with is Ron Dennis. Despite the enormous pressures on his diary and schedule, Ron always made himself available to me. Even if it was for me to express my insecurities and perception of my position in the team, Ron always gave me time. That issue might have been the single most important part of my day, thinking about it, articulating the concern to Ron, hearing his response, analysing that reply; by contrast, his diary would have been crammed with a million other pressing matters, not least running the team and also accommodating another driver with his own concerns and questions. However, with the benefit of being out of that intense fight for a championship, when I look back I can see that Ron must have been so incredibly busy running a business, the race team and everything that goes with being the boss of McLaren, and yet he always made his time available for me. I might only be offered a certain time slot but there was a meeting made available nevertheless. Ron was able to do that because he wanted to, but also because he was extremely good at time management.

This approach could sometimes come across as pretty strict. I remember one morning at a meeting, I turned up and Ron was on the phone so, not wanting to intrude, I said to his secretary, 'I'll just take a wander around and talk to the engineers.' Twenty minutes later, I heard the tannoy telling me to go to Ron's office straight away and when I got there he gave me a right dressing down. 'If we have a ten o'clock meeting, you should be here at ten o'clock.' I explained that I was and that I'd seen him on a call, so I went to use my time in a way that I thought was productive by talking to the engineers. Ron wasn't impressed. 'You don't know when I'm coming off the phone, so you sit there until I'm ready.' You might read from that that he felt he was busier than me, and that was certainly true, but in reality he had so many slots to adhere to each day that if one meeting was 20 minutes late, it could have unhelpful repercussions for everyone else he was due to meet afterwards. The lesson for me was 'don't waste busy people's time'.

As part of his focus on time management, Ron micro-manages his day. So for example, one time we were in a negotiation about a contract renewal, important stuff for an F1 driver, and I made my argument a few times for certain key elements and then suddenly, politely but firmly, Ron said, 'DC, you've made your point, now move on.' We can get so fixated on what's important to us that in our nervousness we find lots of different ways of saying the same thing over and over again. So just be economical, clear and never repetitive. Make your point and move on, like Ron says. Think about it from Ron's point of view: he was running a multi-million-pound engineering and technology company that happens to build hugely successful racing cars and more latterly road cars, too. He can't spend all day with me because otherwise that would be at the expense of other key decisions, so if I was going on too much he would interject, not to be rude or domineering, but to make the very most out of the time he was talking to me.

Another lesson I learnt from working with highly successful people such as Ron, Jackie Stewart and Frank Williams is that you have two ears but only one mouth. Use them proportionately. Listen more than you talk. You might think that hugely influential and successful people such as these famous racers and team managers do all the talking, but in reality they are very good listeners. You might find yourself in a meeting with Frank and he will hardly say a word. However, he will be taking it all in, absorbing the information being presented, processing the best course of action. Being the loudest and most vocal is not necessarily a good asset. Ahead of the 1994 season, I was a Williams test driver but the financial pressure of funding my racing career was getting severe. I genuinely felt that another season in F3000 as a competitive racer would make me a better driver. I honestly believed in my heart that it would also be of benefit to the Williams team if I raced for a further season in Formula 3000, making me a better test and race driver for them. So I put on my best suit and went to see Frank. He was used to seeing his Scottish test driver in casual clothes, so when I walked in all smart he was immediately suspicious and said, 'What are you wearing a suit for, David?' I proceeded to explain my theory and how my racing another season in F3000 would be of great mutual benefit. I did waffle a little (because I was nervous) until eventually Frank broke his silence, interjected and said, 'What is it that you are actually asking me?' I was reaching out to him to help underwrite my career so I said, 'I'd like you to sponsor me for next season in F3000 please.'

Frank's reply?

'No.'

End of conversation. Aware there was no point reiterating or explaining my proposal again, I simply said, 'Thank you very much for your time', and left. Short and sweet.

Know when to listen and when to walk away. Know when to stop talking. That was a moment to stop talking. Frank had made his decision, he wasn't going to change his mind by me repeating myself and taking up even more of his precious time. So, I knew it was time to retreat and find another way.

So as part of your efficiency drive, listen more. You are engaging more with someone by listening to them than talking over them. Strong personalities know what they want to say and when they speak, out of respect of their achievements and their position, you listen. It is a very poor flaw to talk over people; there is an assumption that you know everything they are going to say and more, and then you jump in and often belittle or contradict what they said. Children often do this because they are excited and want to join in, but as an adult you can't do that. Pause, don't jump in, listen, and listen *properly*, not just as a token gesture. It's quite a skill to sit and properly listen to people.

Another expression I learnt from Ron was, 'It's better to keep your mouth closed and let people think you are stupid, than to open it and confirm that you are.' We had a meeting once with a member of a Middle Eastern royal family, and this one man just sat there quietly, soaking it all in, barely saying a word. Afterwards, I mentioned this to Ron and he said, 'He doesn't say much but don't be fooled, when he does it is absolutely worth listening.'

Picking up on this simple truth about efficiency, have you noticed how much absolute waffle people talk in business? Of course, there are certainly some industries where there is a lot of vocabulary that doesn't relate to everyday life, where jargon is necessary. For example, if I was selling cutting-edge medical equipment to the world's most advanced surgeons, then it is clear you'd need to use the correct technical wording. However, in the world where most of us operate, simple, clean and easy-to-understand language can sometimes be hard to find.

You see this in F1. People pick up on what I call 'internal terminology', perhaps because it makes them feel clever, or maybe part of an inner circle? I'm not sure why. Unless that wording is efficient and relevant, then it's essentially just for show.

Here's another example from F1. In my personal opinion, being a race driver is not that difficult or complicated. What you're driving is essentially just a vehicle that will not move until you push the throttle, and if it gets a bit scary or if you think you don't have enough grip, then you lift off the throttle and push the brake. It's a very straightforward, stop, go, left pedal, right pedal. That's all it is, but some people can talk about it as if it were the most complicated science ever invented. I have a racing driver buddy who can explain a qualifying lap at great length and make it sound like some magical,

God-inspired journey of discovery and jeopardy. The reality is that lap probably took 80 seconds because that's how long an average lap will be, during which time there were a lot of straights, so the actual time the driver is 'working' is probably only 20 seconds of an 80-second lap – the rest of the time you are just sitting on the straight. If you actually break a Grand Prix lap down, our input and the key decision points are very small. That is not to say your influence on the race result can't be very significant, it can. So why does it take him so long to describe that lap? There's just no need. To me that's inefficient language.

I sit in so many meetings or listen to very long presentations that are just overly wordy and complicated, where someone is presenting and using all the 'buzz' jargon of that moment, much of which is absolute nonsense, of course. When people talk in abbreviations or acronyms, it's just illustrating that they know something and they think you don't. In fact, often you do know exactly what they are banging on about, but the idea is hidden by all the pointless, verbal showing off. Keep things simple. It's more efficient and less pretentious.

To be fair, sometimes it isn't driven quite so much by ego, it can be a question of pitching at the wrong level – certain people in business sometimes use words that are absolutely beautiful for the context and theoretically correct, but just not mainstream or understandable to the audience they're intended for. I always think, *Does it really explain the issue clearly?* If someone uses a word I don't know, I will always just politely stop them and ask what that means. Okay, sometimes you see the disappointment (occasionally disgust!) that you don't know that word but I have no issue with that; if they explain what they just said then I do know. And it might just tip them off that they are not pitching their wording at the level that is correct for the audience. That can be very discombobulating.

This verbal efficiency should extend to your presentations. I groan at some of the overly complicated presentations I've had to sit through, like an enforced endurance event. In any presentation, keep at the very front of your mind your role in that company, or particular project. Then focus on explaining the challenges of being in that position, and detail the need for the support system of the people around you, effectively reaching out to the other people to get additional input and support by making them feel that this project – and their input – is an important part of the overall challenge. Time and time again I sit in meetings and people waffle on for hours but all they're essentially saying is, 'This is what I do, this is why I'm really, really important to the company and aren't you all lucky that I'm working with you all?' Don't do that, strip out your ego, drill down into what the actual issue is, how your role is being challenged to achieve that and what support you might need from your peers to achieve your mutual goal. That's far more efficient.

The same should apply to your communications. I've already mentioned my bugbear about stupidly long emails. It's just as annoying when people don't respond to an email or they take a long time to reply. I admit that not all of my inbox is answered straight away but I do have a system in place that means I reply in the correct order of priority, as much as I possibly can. It's down to simple housekeeping again. File your work well, in a simple system, so you can put your hand on anything at a moment's notice, but also, when you file something, look first at that paperwork or email and analyse where you need to file it. By doing that you are cementing it into your brain and maybe even thinking about some aspect of it.

This efficiency drive should relate to every part of your career or business. One crucial area of business where I find people can be painfully inefficient is in delivering goods or services. It's not rocket science, but it seems to be something that so many companies and people can't do. Don't let people down. *Just do what you say you are going to do – just deliver.* But how many people don't turn up, or don't get back to you or don't deliver what they said they would? It's ridiculous. You often get an email saying they haven't got back to you because they're waiting on someone else first – well, if that's holding the process up, then go and see that person and get it sorted. Like I said, it's not rocket science.

It's not that complicated to have a basic level of business success because people are easily satisfied with just getting what they asked for. If you are in a restaurant and you ask for a margherita pizza and exactly that turns up in a timely fashion, you will be satisfied. In the same way, delivering a multi-million-pound event is a matter of giving the customer what they asked for. Just deliver what you said you were going to, because then it's very difficult for people to be anything other than satisfied.

Some people deliberately play a manipulative game where they offer less than they are capable of, knowing they have room to offer more if it is useful to do so. However, in my opinion, business is not about under-promising and over-delivering. I just think it's more authentic and honest to say, 'This is what I can do, this is when I can do it by, this is how much it will cost', then stick to exactly that. If you do just that, your customers will be very happy. I'm easily satisfied with people just doing what they say they will do. I don't need the hotel manager to take me to my room, I don't need a bottle of champagne in the room at eleven o'clock check-in. I don't remember Karen and I ever opening a bottle of champagne in a hotel room when we've just arrived. Here is the hotel room, it's immaculate as it should be, it costs this much, here is your key. Job done.

Trades are particularly bad for this. Any property project I've done has usually taken considerably more time and cost much more money than was originally forecast; that seems to be almost an accepted mode of operation in the building industry. However, to me that is not acceptable. I can tell you now that I've never been a builder but I do know that making an 800bhp Formula 1 car go round a track quicker than your rivals is more complex than building a simple extension. As I've said before, F1 efficiency means that every Grand Prix will start bang on time. So why can't the joiner turn up at 1pm to fix my door frame?

Another rather ludicrous lack of efficiency is when companies say the phone repair guy will turn up 'between 8am and 6pm'. Imagine if they said that in F1? 'We are thinking of starting the race somewhere between 10am and 5pm, no idea when exactly, and we won't let you know so you've just got to sit in front of your TV all day and wait.' In my view, that's an unacceptable way to treat a customer. It's basically saying, 'We are more important than you, the paying customer.'

Efficiency is usually associated with everything going well. However, this isn't necessarily always the case. For example, everyone experiences times where things don't go to plan. That might be a loss in sports or a business relationship that has gone sour. One investment outside of F1 that I made was in the Columbus Hotel I mentioned before, in Monaco. Although at times this was very enjoyable, ultimately it was a difficult investment and unfortunately ended with legal arguments and I no longer have a good relationship with my partner. Clearly, if there is a serious difference of opinion on something very important, then you have to defend your corner. However, there comes a point where you also need to realise that fighting on and on is detrimental to your progress, even if on paper you might seem to win that battle. There should come a point when

– to use a hotel analogy – you think, *I'm checking out*. If the situation has become a legal issue, then the cost of proving you are right on every single point can be debilitating. You are still right, but if you cut and run at an agreeable point, then you can get on with making new, positive experiences. We are all busy people. As I keep saying, there are only so many hours in a day and you have only so much energy with which to use that time. Just know that sometimes it is the best course of action to cut your losses. That can sometimes be the clever path, and not necessarily the defeatist one. It's about knowing which battles to fight, and for how long.

It *can* be different, things can be more efficient. In Monaco, there is a system where you have a precise time slot for the MOT for your car. If you are five minutes late, your slot will be cancelled and you have to reapply for the next slot, plus you won't be able to use your car in the meantime. Guess what? People just aren't five minutes late. They are always on time. I'm not trying to invent the flying bicycle or some hare-brained idea, here. It's pretty simple stuff.

· · ·

Without efficiency, you or your business will fail to deliver the single most important element of any business: good, old-fashioned customer service. It's called 'service' for a reason and you need to deliver that. Don't make excuses for your company or your performance. On that point, you can help yourself by not over-promising in the first instance. You must apply due diligence in the early stages of a deal or project. Unfortunately, many people commit to something that isn't possible because they are so keen to win a contract or a new job. Again, I can draw lessons from Formula 1 for this. There are many precedents for parts manufacture, so if a particular brake part takes four weeks to build, and assuming that the part hasn't changed that much, then F1 people don't promise it in three weeks. Otherwise they will potentially miss being on the grid; as I said before, the start lights wait for no one. A far better approach is to be completely honest, tell the customer it takes a month and then hit that deadline bang on time. Same amount of time to make the part – one approach is a week late, one is bang on time. One generates repeat business, one doesn't.

What is customer service? It's about looking someone in the eye and making them believe that you care and that you want to deliver on your promises, then actually executing that. I'm going to go slightly off-piste here, but bear with me, it will make for a clear illustration of great customer service. It's a funny story that involves an Irishman, a bottle of whisky and a flight to the UK, but ultimately illustrates how even massive companies can offer fantastic customer service. There are really no excuses.

My wife Karen had gone out for the night to a concert and my Irish friend Harry Gibbings came around to the apartment for a drink while she was out. Harry has recently got into whisky, so I said, 'I've got a wee bar at home', and he joined me for a drink. The whisky we opened was really nice so… anyway, you don't want the details, suffice to say I don't remember how the evening finished but I vaguely remember tidying up the mess before I went to bed.

I'd set my alarm for 5.55am ahead of an early morning flight to the UK. Turns out I slept through the alarm. Luckily Karen's alarm woke me up not much later and she said, 'You've missed your flight!' I replied, 'No, I can get the flight!' to which she replied, 'There's no chance!'

I got dressed and was out of the apartment in a few minutes because I'd packed my case the night before. Taxi across to Nice airport, arriving at 07.40 for a 07.55 flight. So I then had to do the thing that I say I never do, which is to run to the gate at full pelt to see if I could make it. Fortunately, with Nice airport you don't have a 40-minute security lane, and as I'm running through the duty-free, this French BA employee who I've seen for the last 20 years came over and said, 'Bonjour, Monsieur Coulthard, we have been calling you, I told them you've never booked a flight and then not made it before, this was most unusual, I said you would make it…' He ushered me to the gate as I thanked him, I then recognised and also thanked the lady on the gate as I rushed through final checks and made the flight with about ten minutes to spare. I sat down and texted Karen, 'Made the flight. x'. She texted back, 'You jammy *******. x'.

The point I'm trying to make here is not that you shouldn't finish a bottle of good whisky the night before an early flight, nor is it that I have a very patient wife, but that the customer service that the British Airways crew member showed was just amazing. Yes, I've been catching flights through Nice airport for 20 years and, okay, maybe my face is reasonably well known in certain circles, but that guy had taken the time to notice my patterns of arrival, timings etc., and he felt that it was unlikely I would just be a no-show. He then went to his superiors and said he felt they should assume I would make it and they took that advice and acted upon it. I often make fun of the French because Karen is half-French and I rib her that they are always on strike and all that, just to be silly, but that day was just all about incredible customer service. Credit where credit is due, that's 20-plus years of building a relationship that has got me on a flight back to London when I should have missed it. No hint of 'Computer says no' or 'You're too late, sorry', they just thought ahead, acted on their knowledge and delivered for the customer. I made the flight but only because the customer service of BA – a huge organisation – was exemplary.

Just to neatly and completely contradict my actual behaviour above, this story does allow me to make a point about allowing room for problems in your schedule planning in order to keep you being always efficient. If it is a time-critical event or meeting, I tend not to take the last flight possible, just to give myself the space. It's a pretty basic idea, but if I take the second-last flight then if there is a problem with mine, I still have a chance to make the meeting.

Simple planning, isn't it? Hoping for the best and preparing for the worst. I never understand people who arrive 40 minutes late for a meeting and say there was traffic or a delay somewhere. If it takes an hour to get to your meeting then don't just allow an hour or an hour and five minutes. Leave room. If you are late, then how can you be efficient, how can you provide good customer service if you're not there on time?

Getting back to my point about customer service, there is nothing better than being dealt with by someone who clearly cares about you as a customer, who makes sure that your experience is a positive one and gives you a standard of service that makes you want more. Underlining the earlier point about the importance of listening, this skill is particularly important when dealing with customers. Customer service isn't just about being proactive. At times it is as much about reacting to the customer than anything else. There's the clichéd image of a salesman, this gift-of-the-gab-style character, with an answer for everything and talking at a million miles an hour. However, if you don't listen to what the customer is saying, how will you know what they want? This comes down to ego and awareness of your customer. Don't kid yourself that if you're not talking, you're not looking after the customer. Sometimes listening is far more important.

Customer service is also very much about responding to customer demands – a fact of business that is just as important in F1 as in any industry because, in reality, we are all providing customer service. As an example, let's look at the current demand for more environmentally friendly automotive technologies, particularly in hybrid power trains, and finding ways to make fuel help us to go further than ever before. Today's Formula 1 engines are the most efficient internal combustion engines ever produced, with Mercedes now claiming 50 per cent thermal efficiency, which compares to the less than 35 per cent thermal efficiency for road car engines. This has translated into almost 1000bhp from the tiny 1.6 litre V6 petrol-electric hybrid power units in use today, using 100 kilos of fuel per race instead of the 160 kilos which was common up until 2013; on top of that the leading teams are using only three engines per driver per season. This compares to an engine per day back in the early 1990s.

By 2014/15 we were able to produce over 800bhp and cover the race distance of 300km at the same speed, but using 35 to 40 per cent less fuel thanks to using a tiny engine mated to a large electric motor which will be powered by a range of energy recovery systems including an advanced 'e'-turbo which uses waste gases to charge the battery. Our critics might point out that Formula 1 is polluting the atmosphere, but when you consider that one transatlantic flight generates more pollution than an entire season of Formula 1, it makes the criticism less valid.

This is all very geeky and fascinating but the point I want to make is that F1 headed down this path partly as a response to customer demands. The development of the petrol-electric turbocharged hybrid move was in response to car industry demand at a time when the world's leading automotive manufacturers are moving away from large capacity, fuel-hungry internal combustion engines.

I hope that all these examples illustrate how crucial efficiency and customer service can make the difference between a successful business and one that simply collapses. If we go back to my writer friend who had the bad experience at the car dealership, what they did there was take a pleasurable life experience and turn it into a very unpleasant moment. How is that good customer service? Maybe I am demanding because I'm used to great customer service when my pit-lane crew can change my tyres in three seconds, but once you have experienced world-class customer service it's only natural to aspire to the same.

· · ·

I'd like to close this chapter by using an example of a business I am involved in to illustrate the benefits of efficiency and customer service. In January 2017 I co-founded Velocity Experience with Guy Horner. Guy is the brother of my old team principal Christian Horner, and is a highly successful executive in the events management industry and the chief executive of TBA plc

I'd been thinking about that idea for some time. You might ask why I wanted to be in the event space when I already have my TV work, a production company called Whisper Films (which I will come to shortly) and brand ambassador roles to keep me very busy. Well, I'm surrounded by events all the time, I am constantly attending them, being involved with presenting them sometimes, it is just a regular part of my world. The companies I work with such as UBS and Heineken all use events to sculpt, shape and create experiences for their customers. At that level, these big businesses all have agencies that are creating events for them and some of those agencies are very good. However, as I said before, very good is not enough; you have to be exceptional. I saw there was a space for me to be involved with my own business and I felt that if I found the right people, we could do a first-class, efficient job and provide a world-class service.

After I was introduced to Guy, it immediately became apparent that our respective skills and contacts could work well together. When I met Guy, the ideas in my head started to crystallise. We set Velocity up and that was all relatively straightforward. Guy wasn't focused on motorsport particularly but he offered an absolute turnkey – and efficient – solution because he already had the creativity and the staff while I had the contacts who could open the doors to new opportunities. His experience gave us credibility to say, 'This is what we have done before within the group', and my experience allowed us to be talking to people inside motorsport who were able to make decisions. Guy had the experience, the infrastructure and the reputation already established within that area and that provided us with the potential to leverage my contacts and knowledge of motorsport to deliver a great service.

We launched Velocity at the end of January 2017 and I invited the new head of F1, Chase Carey, who represented the new owners of the sport, Liberty Media, to a launch we held in London at a nice Michelin-star restaurant. He came along with some other people who might be potential customers and clients for Velocity. We knew that Liberty Media were looking at doing some high-impact events, including talk of a showcase London event. At a follow-up meeting with the commercial director of F1, Sean Bratches, we said, 'We can do the London event.' He asked us for a price. My partner Guy, who understands that side of the business intimately, told him what he believed the cost would be, and at that moment Sean reached over the table and said, 'If you can do it for that price, you've got a deal.' We shook hands and that was it, we'd secured the deal. We then delivered that event at exactly the price we had agreed.

That event was F1 Live London. The aim was to bring Formula 1 closer to its fans, and I think we can say we did that – 100,000 people flooded into Trafalgar Square to meet Formula 1 racing's teams and drivers, complemented by an exhibition beforehand at the British Grand Prix at Silverstone. In London, we put on live car demonstrations in Whitehall, three headline music acts – Little Mix, Bastille and the Kaiser Chiefs – and loads of activities for schools (under the umbrella of 'F1 in Schools', a not-for-profit company established in 2000 to give an opportunity for students to learn about STEM-related subjects). I'm very proud to say that the event was a huge success and has since won five major awards, including 'The Sports Event of the Year'. Remember – this was Velocity's first ever project.

Velocity has worked very well so far and is a new business that I am extremely pleased to be involved with. And if you strip it back to why it is successful, aside from our respective contacts and experience, it is because when we agree to provide an event, we efficiently deliver exactly what we said we would while providing exemplary customer service. That's the driving force behind the company.

To sum up my thoughts about efficiency, consider Formula 1 again: if you take the 'perfect' F1 race, when all the teams, drivers, mechanics, suppliers and everyone else involved in putting those 20 cars out on track all do their job efficiently, then in fact there is a very good chance that the race will be criticised for being boring. Without failures, there might be no overtaking; without incident there might be a predictable procession. No one will crash, no parts will fail and no team strategies will be wrong. The grid will all go round the circuit safely and neatly and get to the end in the same order. It is harsh on F1 that when that happens – essentially when the sport is achieving its peak performance – it is seen as not entertaining. In the perfect racing scenario, nothing happens out of the ordinary. So in that sense, Formula 1 is a contradiction because it is so focused on efficiency as a goal and yet the ultimate manifestation of that, using the current circuits and cars, is an uneventful race.

In business you don't want incidents, if they can be avoided. You want a business flight to be unremarkable, efficient. Take off on time, have clear air, land on time so that you can get to your meeting punctually. There are so many things in life where you want that to be the case but in the business of sport, people also want entertainment. The boxer who misses the big right hand coming in, the footballer who misses an open goal, the athlete who suffers a hamstring pull in the home straight, these all create tension, moments of drama, this is why people watch sport.

In business, you don't want that. You want efficiency, you want to provide the customer with exactly what they expect or ask for – and that has to start with yourself.

CHAPTER 9
THE UNFAIR ADVANTAGE

I mentioned earlier that Jackie Stewart says he always felt he had a competitive advantage over other people in business because of his sporting background. I quite like that. He is right, the sense of driven, hard-working individuals striving to be the best, the intense teamwork, the precision, attention to detail and efficiency, the culture of constant evolution and improvement, all these ideas are so ingrained in racing drivers, and sportspeople generally. As I have hopefully explained a little in this book, F1 taught me so many of these skills that I have tried to transfer to business. I do that because I want to come first, I don't want to do well but be second or third. That ultra-competitive streak doesn't really go away, it might dilute slightly with age – for some – but it is always there. Sportspeople will always want to win.

For my part, as far as forging a post-F1 career, I was aware that I was not the only retired F1 driver out there, I know who my competitors are in the world of motorsport TV. It amazes me when

I meet people in business who aren't that up to speed with what their competitors are doing. How can that be? In Formula 1, there is an almost fanatical interest in what other teams are doing because part of the innovation race in Formula 1 is to watch and understand how rivals are evolving their technologies and interpreting the rules. In Formula 1, our competition is right beside us in the pit lane. We see our competitors and we shake hands with them. They try to take sneaky peeks at our car. They talk to us. Teams scrutinise each other in extreme detail, employing full-time photographers to take high-definition images of rival cars, and using all the available means in terms of video and even audio to work out what the competition is up to (sound analysis of engine and exhaust notes can be used to figure out rpm and road speed, which enables teams to be able to see comparative speed traces). Teams cannot develop their cars in isolation, and understanding the competitive landscape is essential. What the other guys are doing, how and why, is part of the game. The same should apply to you.

It's not just about the business traits that F1 teaches you, though. It's also the post-career opportunities. I would expand on what Jackie suggests and say that sport has fast-tracked me to the boardroom of many companies around the world, it has enabled me to meet CEOs of huge global corporations and major business players. These super-achievers are used to being the boss of companies that might employ thousands, or even hundreds of thousands of people. Their business world is their empire and they rule that domain. However, when they come to the track, they are coming into my world, and that position of absolute authority is stripped away. That's not me saying I want to bring them down a peg or two, what I mean by that is that even the most successful CEO with a reputation for being a hard-nosed business-type can be suddenly almost child-like in their joy at standing in a garage in the pit lane next to an F1 car when the engineers start up that monstrously loud and powerful engine. This pure sense of joy and wonder sweeps over them and it's very disarming in a good way – because it allows you to see the human under the stern business persona. So from that point of view, I have been fortunate to be around these very successful people in an environment that I am familiar with and they are not.

Conversely, though, I would suggest that sometimes being an ex-Formula 1 racer is not a passport to guaranteed post-racing income. Jackie's view about sportspeople having an unfair advantage is not universally accepted. It has been suggested by some that as a career, being an F1 driver is effectively a suspended childhood washed around with millions of pounds, and therefore it is a recipe for creating a disastrous business life after the 200mph days have stopped. There is no retired racing drivers' manual explaining what we should do, you have no real guidance. You can talk to other drivers, but they are all different people. So to some degree I would agree that we are stepping into the unknown.

One problem for high-profile sportspeople and celebrities is that very often their entire sporting life is micro-managed. From the moment they wake up to the time they go back to sleep, they have people organising and managing their day, from big events such as actual races to tiny details such as paperwork, finances and so on. This has become a necessity for many because the demands on their time dictate that they simply do not have the hours in the day, nor the skill set required, to look through dozens of contracts, file accounts, negotiate terms and so on. I know from a pal who works in the music industry that some very famous pop stars sometimes have spreadsheets with their entire year ahead segmented into 15-minute slots, already filled in. However, when the career is over, that spreadsheet is empty or, more likely, doesn't even exist.

During these high-profile, super-hectic careers, this intense micro-management is generally a good thing, although it must feel incredibly claustrophobic at times. The problem comes when the sports or entertainment career ends. At that point, they might still have a large financial portfolio, maybe investments or properties or perhaps designs on going into business. The problem is, they may not be personally capable of doing any of that. There may no longer be anyone there to micro-manage their world. Then it can fall apart very quickly, and if the sums involved are big, it can go horribly wrong. I know guys who have stopped racing who haven't really got into anything else, either because they are not motivated, or they don't need to financially, and if their personality isn't suitable, that can be a recipe for disaster. You sometimes see famous sportsmen or celebrities being declared bankrupt, but in my eyes that doesn't diminish the achievements which they are famous for – they're still champions – it just means that they have not been as successful outside of their field with other avenues they pursued. There are many rather sad stories of failure and downward spirals with former sportspeople. The problem is, as far as getting help or guidance, you can see why there wouldn't be much sympathy for a multi-millionaire playboy racing driver who is struggling to come to terms with his podium-winning career being over.

Acknowledging that this can be the case, I would still side with Sir Jackie and also add the suggestion that I believe the fortunes of sportspeople after their first career ends is perhaps more down to their personal make-up than the legacy of their sporting world. You have to make your own way.

• • •

I am now involved in hotel ownership, film and media, as well as various other businesses. In a sense, it has been almost a continuation of my racing career – of course, my main job as a racing driver is very specific and totally different from any of the above, but there are similarities and I feel lucky that I have been equipped with those skills and then found areas where I can use them.

Why would I go off into completely different arenas, starting from scratch, when there are rich pickings within my current world that I continue to operate in now, ten years after retirement? It would've been far easier to just take a job in a team or a simpler role anywhere in another formula, because coming from the pinnacle of motorsport, any successful former F1 driver is a sought-after commodity within the sport.

For my way of thinking and ambition, that's just too limiting. The downside of that approach is that you can't physically be in two places at once; my business as an individual or sports personality in terms of television and brand contracts is not scalable. If Ferrari want an ex-driver to consult for them, he can't be doing that for McLaren, too. Similarly, outside of motorsport, if one company wants me in Dubai for an event, I can't also be in New York the same night for another company. So I was aware when I finished racing that making a living from just being a former racing driver was not going to be enough. I needed to find new avenues that were scalable, that didn't just rely on my name or reputation.

I am lucky to have earned well during my time in F1 but regardless of my financial position, I definitely have the motivation to keep pushing and look for opportunity and work because I enjoy the whole process. And, fortunately, in my opinion, if you make the most of the opportunities and circumstances that F1, and elite sport, puts you in, then like Jackie before me, I would suggest it gives us an unfair advantage. Therefore, it would be taking that head start for granted to not make the very most out of that privileged position.

. . .

There is nothing that I have done that has been ground-breaking. I haven't invented the iPhone or some revolutionary new product. What I'd humbly suggest I've been quite adept at doing is taking all the exacting lessons of a life in Formula 1 that we've talked about in this book and applying them in the world of business. At times, I have been amazed how few of them are already in use.

With this in mind, I'd like to use as an example Whisper Films, a production company that I helped set up in 2009 with the well-known TV presenter Jake Humphrey and Sunil Patel, a TV executive I'd come across during his time working at the BBC. I'd like to discuss that project, hopefully as a good illustration of how applying F1-style approaches to various areas of business can give you an unfair advantage.

I didn't know I'd end up being involved in a production company; however, that became clear to me when I saw how television operated and how disconnected it was from the attention to detail I was used to. TV is an incredible industry but lacking a lot of structure. Specifically, after I did my first BBC gig in 2009 in Melbourne, I went back and said, 'Right, are we going to have a debrief to discuss some of the problems we had as a team? I'd like to talk about the mistakes I made and the missed opportunities and technical difficulties with the equipment', but they said, 'No, we don't do that sort of thing.' I was amazed; this was completely alien to me. Coming from an F1 background with the level of self-analysis that I have explained earlier, this was completely surprising to me that we wouldn't sit down as a team and discuss where mistakes were made. It wasn't about wanting to point fingers but, as I said above, out of your mistakes come your biggest opportunities. If you fix the problem that could have been a mission critical issue, then it puts you a step ahead of the competition. That day was the moment that I started to think about setting up a TV production company.

I'd previously met Jake in Shanghai in 2008 when he was on a fact-finding mission for the BBC's forthcoming F1 broadcast team. I first worked with him in Melbourne the following year. Sunil was working with the BBC on the production side. Very quickly, I saw how good these two men were. Jake and Sunil had themselves been having the conversation about doing something in this space, and I said, 'If you do it, I'm with you, absolutely.' We talked about our goals and decided that a key target was to one day broadcast Formula 1, no small-scale ambition for a new TV production company that didn't even exist yet.

You might ask, what was it in Sunil and Jake that attracted me to working with them? Firstly Sunil: his attention to detail, the way he runs the business, is amazing. Even his notepad, his writing in there is immaculate, his planning, his precision makes him a standout person in that industry. As for Jake, he is a very focused, energetic, committed, experienced television presenter with great credibility. He came from children's television then through sport at the BBC and that led to him getting a presenting role at the newly formed BT Sport TV channel. He has different skills from both Sunil and myself, and he clearly understands television. Jake is also a very good networker, he's a very social individual, so all of those assets are very powerful for Whisper. Jake talks to individuals that he comes across during the course of his travels around the UK attending various events and that generates some really interesting projects. So the three of us have different ways of dealing with people but I think we complement each other.

When I was racing, I tried to surround myself with the best mechanics and the best engineers, to work with the best and create opportunities. That's exactly what I realised I could do with Whisper. I saw in those two men a range of abilities that I felt would be a huge boost for any production company. These included many skills that I do not have. Likewise, I knew that with them alongside me, I could create business and client opportunities that as a team we could exploit. If I am out and about, I'm constantly looking for opportunities and feeding them back. So, we all have a clear role. It's empowering the team and then getting on with it. Trust the team to deliver. I was working with brands that would give us an opportunity because they trusted in me. Building long-term relationships is based on trust. Trust that you will turn up and do the job that's expected of you, that you will deliver, for as long as it is expected. Sunil has got the keys to the business, Jake and I aren't in the office every day, it is Sunil driving the business forward, but we are equal partners. I have total trust in him and without that trust it wouldn't work.

In return, there is a large element of trust from Sunil. He has gone from being salaried at the BBC to being the MD and a shareholder in one of the fastest growing independent sports production companies out there. In theory, that was a risk for him. However, Jake and Sunil never had any doubt that if they needed funding, I would find a solution, they trusted in my ability to do that. As it happens, it has never been the case that we have needed a great deal of funding because we've been cash positive from the very beginning. Nonetheless, my involvement gave them that confidence to go out and get the business, knowing that if funding was needed, it would be there. I was prepared to invest a large sum into Whisper because looking at the opportunity that seemed like a wise thing to do. As it happened, my investment was able to be much more modest because we quite literally got off to a flyer.

We started with small steps – no massive, flash office, just a small, rented studio in Ealing, no bigger than a small kitchen. I don't believe in these businesses that are 'all flash and no dash', huge overheads, all for show, yet no clients. There has to be substance behind the presentation. So at the start of Whisper it was really as simple as understanding the costs and living within our means.

The hardest job in any new company is to gain the first traction, to win initial recognition and credibility – that takes time and effort and belief and real commitment, but once you've won that you can be creative, grow and build the business from there. Our first contract was a branded product for Williams but since then we have gone on to work with the likes of UBS, Hugo Boss, Heineken, producing the NFL show for BBC, women's rugby, women's football, documentaries and all sorts of branded content, but the jewel in the crown for us all was winning the Formula 1 production on behalf of Channel 4 Television. If a pitch presents itself, then we all work very hard on that idea.

At the time of writing, we employ around 40 people and have had to move to bigger offices twice due to the rate of expansion, but it's not about the money for me, it's about trying to build Whisper into something even bigger. Of course, once you achieve your goal, you shouldn't rest on your laurels and become complacent. Our new aim is to continue to grow revenue streams, diversify, we are looking into maybe Whisper Talent, which would oversee management contracts for the creative individuals who are part of the media.

The best example of how Whisper has succeeded by using F1 lessons is when we won that contract to produce the Channel 4 coverage of Formula 1, hopefully another interesting example of many of the topics discussed in this book. By 2015, I was a retired racing driver commentating on the Formula 1 coverage on the BBC. Meanwhile, over at *Top Gear*, the departure of Jeremy Clarkson, Richard Hammond and James May from the BBC's flagship programme led to much rumour about who was going to become one of the new presenters. In many ways, this was a huge opportunity for any presenter, although there were certainly those who felt it might also be a poisoned chalice given the phenomenal success of the previous presenting team – in essence, how do you follow that?

I got a call late in December saying they were putting together a new team for *Top Gear*, including Chris Evans, and that my name was in the ring. I heard that everyone and their dog was contacting the BBC asking about the vacancies, which is understandable, so I was very flattered to have my name considered. However, I didn't contact them, just like when Senna was killed and I never contacted Frank; rather different, obviously, but I just feel sometimes if you know you are potentially involved, it can be just as powerful not to dash in shouting how brilliantly ideal you are. However, for certain I was interested, it was potentially a massive opportunity, *Top Gear* is absolutely huge around the world. Yes, I was a little nervous about the scope for rejection, those three former presenters were immensely popular and were a tough act to follow, but I was still very interested indeed.

I met with the team down at the BBC – bear in mind I was contracted to the BBC at this point – and without wishing to go into all the private detail, we were pretty advanced in our agreement. Then the BBC announced that they were relinquishing the rights to broadcast Formula 1. Channel 4 would be taking over. How did this affect me? Well, when we started Whisper, one of the absolute goals was to eventually secure the rights to Formula 1 for British broadcast. The reason we put the effort in all those years ago was to build something up such that one day we would be broadcasting Formula 1. We wanted to be the biggest sports production company in the UK. That was our goal and we had a strategy to achieve it. You can't say that and not mean it.

However, clearly I couldn't work for the BBC and also Channel 4 with Whisper at the same time. Formula 1 coverage takes around 60 days of my year, which doesn't sound like a lot, but when you add to that all the travelling and prep, it is a big commitment. Likewise, *Top Gear* is a complex and exhaustive programme to produce, so that is another huge commitment. I had to make a decision and choose one or the other.

I decided to go with Whisper and go all out to win the Formula 1 pitch. That was a risk but in my view the correct decision. This was right before Christmas and the pitch was due on 4 January. I was up in Switzerland with Karen and I said, 'I'm really sorry, but this is a mammoth opportunity, Christmas has just been cancelled, sorry.' Over the next couple of weeks, despite the time of year, we pulled together all the key people we would need to prove we could do this broadcast. Some of these people turned down other work to join the pitch, even though there was no guarantee we would win. That is commitment and risk!

Channel 4 were brilliant but they did stipulate that I could not be working for the BBC on *Top Gear* as well as doing their F1 coverage. That was fair enough. However, despite the BBC no longer doing F1, I still had a contract with them for a few years yet. So I had to negotiate being released out of that contract, such was my commitment to Whisper. I paid around £30,000 in legal fees out of my own pocket to make sure it was all done correctly and to make sure this could happen. I could have got Whisper to contribute towards the legal costs because it was to their benefit but I didn't because I could afford to pay that myself, and I wanted to show my partners that my commitment was absolute. Sometimes you need to be prepared to show just how committed you are, and that can mean getting out your wallet. I even had my lawyer, who is based in Australia, sleeping in his spare room so he could work on British time. Again, commitment.

So after a hectic Christmas of very long hours and virtually no time off, we did the pitch, we won the contract and Whisper achieved its goal of becoming an F1 broadcaster. It was never a given, there were some great production companies after that contract, obviously, and many TV agents would no doubt argue that the *Top Gear* role would've been a higher profile and potentially better choice. However, that was what I was committed to and that is what I did. So were my team, and every person was a crucial cog in that process. That teamwork, commitment and diligence paid off. We had set that Formula 1 contract as a goal and worked towards that as a coherent team. So when we did eventually win the Formula 1 contract it was not a surprise to any of us, because we'd spoken about it as a very clear goal. Looking back, we are incredibly proud that all those years previously, Jake, Sunil and I had stood in Melbourne and said, 'Let's do this, let's build Whisper and one day we'll do Formula 1.' That's exactly what we did. By applying many of the lessons that all three of us had learnt in Formula 1, we set up the company, got off to a flyer and then won the ultimate prize, the broadcast rights to F1. Considering that sport was in so many ways the guiding light to show us how to operate, there was a fantastic sense of coming full circle in securing that significant achievement.

CHAPTER 10
A FEW CLOSING THOUGHTS

In this book I have tried to draw lessons from Formula 1 that I believe can benefit people in business. However, I would also like to append these ideas with a few that are not motorsport lessons, but essentially just my views on life and business.

Firstly – and I make this point fully recognising that I have been involved in a very well-paid job for a number of years – money should not always be the motivating factor alone for your business or career decisions. As I say, you might criticise me because I have earned good money racing, and I accept that, but the sentiment remains: money is a motivation but assuming that you have achieved a certain level of financial security – you can put food on the table, buy clothes, pay for a house and car – then to a degree the journey and the experience are just as important. At the end of the day, why do any of these super-wealthy achievers continue to work long hours on very demanding projects? Why not retire and sit on a beach? Why does a multi-millionaire still go into work? Well, some people choose to sunbathe their days away, of course, but many more are bored at just the thought of that, which proves that success is as much about the experience and the challenge as it is the financial rewards. The bonus is that if you can make your project or career an enjoyable challenge, then you will undoubtedly be better at it – and if that happens, the likelihood is that the money will come anyway.

When I sat and listened to will.i.am at that business conference, talking about how he isn't afraid of going back to the projects, because that was a place full of love and a happy life, he also made some very pertinent points about the topic of money versus enjoyment. Like me, he believes that if you can do what you do for *fun*, then it will be both more enjoyable and also – more likely than not – profitable. He makes music because he loves making music. Similarly, despite all the complexity of being a Formula 1 driver, I raced for fun. I didn't race for money but I did get paid.

It's not about being a sportsperson, it's not about earning loads of money or being the richest business person, it's about feeling that you have got a task to get on with, doing that as best as you can and then moving on to the next challenge, whether that's cleaning my kart as a 12-year-old lad or testing an F1 car or going to a crucial business conference.

I don't think I am disqualified from having a view on motivation versus money just because I was a very well-paid driver – when I was in the paddock racing, if you had offered me the choice of either the Mercedes car that Lewis Hamilton drives with no wages or a healthy wage with a car from lower down the grid, it would be a no brainer: get me the Mercedes!

My next personal suggestion might sound a little old-fashioned to some of the more cut-throat people out there, and picks up on something I mentioned in Chapter 2. It is simply the notion of playing by the rules of decency and fairness. The modern world of business and sport can both certainly be very ruthless, but for me the basic values of decency and civility remain relevant. Formula 1 is renowned for people making what appear to be very ruthless decisions. However, no matter how harsh the environment you are operating in, that doesn't mean that you can bend the rules to get the win. Sport is defined by rules and regulations. It's not lawless, it's not the Wild West – even though sometimes some drivers' overtaking moves might suggest otherwise! Each sport has a set of rules and competitors abide by them – they might not agree with them, as proven by the almost perennial controversy and discussion about certain F1 rules – but if you want to race in F1, that is the rule book. The same should apply in business – play by the rules. People throw around phrases such as 'all's fair in love and war' and similar excuses for cheating or working outside of the rules, but for me where is the pride in that?

Another personal preference – albeit one that I know has probably been fuelled by F1 – is my fondness to travel and explore.

Even though I was born in a small rural village, I always knew I wanted to travel. I was always motivated to get out and discover. As a youngster I never thought I would be with the girl next door, so there is no surprise that I'm married to a foreigner. I always felt I was going to travel, I never felt like I was going to buy the house next door. That's not to suggest that staying close to your roots is inferior, it absolutely isn't – my brother lives in the house next door to my parents, and has a happily fulfilled life, loves his family, loves his work, and is a very successful haulier through and through. In fact, that passion is why I think the family business continues to sustain.

Travel is not for everyone, of course, but for me I just had this wanderlust to discover the wider world and for a long time my racing career allowed me that privilege. That has carried on after I retired from racing – for example, during the week I was writing this chapter, I wasn't able to work on the book much because I went to Nice/Dubai/Bali for one night and then Bali/Dubai/Brazil for three nights and then Brazil/Barcelona for a night and then back home. I've looked back at my diary for 2017 and I took 159 flights.

At the time of writing, I will have been on a world tour for 25 years as a Formula 1 driver and beyond. Not even the Rolling Stones have done a tour that long! So many of the biggest opportunities come from the diverse group of people I meet as I travel around and I admit I am very lucky because Formula 1 attracts hugely interesting people from all sorts of incredible industries. So if you have to travel with work, or indeed choose to travel for pleasure, make the most of it. You can meet some amazing individuals and, if your eyes and ears are open, you can learn so much.

Some people question why I need to keep earning money as I must have done well out of Formula 1 and my other businesses and, to a degree, I understand that. I have earned well on occasion. However, resting on my financial laurels is not how my mind operates. I tend not to look at what I have in terms of properties, stocks, shares, investment income. I tend to look at 'What is my potential income this year?' I have unfortunately experienced the changing fortunes of investing in the stock markets – one day you're sitting pretty thinking, *Aren't I clever?* then overnight you've lost a significant amount, often due to forces you had no control over.

While we are on that topic, I'd like to make the point that there is a crucial difference between losing money and spending money. People might look at certain items you've bought and say, 'Why do you need that?' However, the point is, if you've earned that money through hard work and creativity, then you've earned the right to spend it how you please. That is very different from losing money on investments. There is no way that I would be in a business that is losing money. I just don't see the sense or the point, it completely goes against the grain. That's where I find it difficult to comprehend all these start-ups, often internet companies, that are losing millions and millions every year, not making a profit for years, and yet they have these massive inflated market values. That's just alien to me. That is part of my drive to set up new businesses and sensibly and progressively make them profitable.

One characteristic that I have always been lucky enough to possess even before I was involved in Formula 1 is self-belief. I always felt confident that if I worked hard enough and applied all the ideas I've spoken about, I could make something of myself. My father had enormous belief in my motor-racing potential; as I've said, he used to say things like, 'When you are in F1, I think you should move to Monaco', way back when I was in my early teens. Not 'if' but 'when'. I guess that must have rubbed off on me.

F1 then put me in circles where I met many, many individuals with, quite frankly, *enormous* levels of self-belief (top sportspeople are like that, it's not just motorsport). This personality trait is also not just restricted to the drivers either – team managers, mechanics and various other people within the paddock possess great confidence and self-belief.

For my part, absolute self-belief was at the very core of what I did as a Formula 1 racing driver. Sitting in my 800bhp, 200mph car, racing other guys who were equally determined – and sometimes a little bit crazy – I had to spend around one hour and 40 minutes pushing myself and the equipment to its limit. I can only see the track directly in front of me, and maybe a little bit of colour of the car behind in my wing mirrors. Other than that, it's the steering wheel in my hands. So I need total belief in my abilities out there on track.

This is as it should be because to succeed at the top level, I think you unreservedly have to have the strength of your conviction. Sometimes, however, that conviction gets blurred with an almost clinical sense of what is about to happen. Prior to the French Grand Prix in 2000, I somehow *knew* I was going to win. I knew I had the car and team to take the chequered flag. Even in qualifying, when I was forced to use the team's spare car because of a technical problem, I was able to out-qualify my teammate Mika Häkkinen and qualify second on the grid beside Michael Schumacher's Ferrari.

When I woke up on that Sunday morning I remember doing a little bit of training on my rowing machine and feeling totally confident that this would be my day. In the race, that's exactly what happened, because even after I dropped to third place at the start, I was able to overtake Rubens Barrichello in his Ferrari, catch Michael and then overtake him after a good battle for several laps. I had the certainty I could win, the team supporting me in the pits – everything fell into place. Before the Monaco Grand Prix in 2002, I had the same feeling and even got my victory kilt out of the wardrobe beforehand. I absolutely believed I was going to win that Grand Prix, too.

Self-belief is so crucial in business. You have to believe in what you are saying. You have to believe in what you are selling, what you are trying to achieve, that will come across. Conversely, if you don't really believe in and feel your product or project, people will sniff that out.

You shouldn't be blind about your ideas, though. There is a balance – if no one else in the world agrees with you, then it might be wise to take a step back and review your position. That said, there are many stories in business, sport and life where someone has been a lone believer and ends up being proved correct. My mother is a bit like that, she can argue that white is black because she said it's black, she can be very committed! In business, though, joking aside, that strength of conviction has held her and my father in good stead.

You have to be careful that self-belief doesn't tip into arrogance or complacency. That in turn will blunt your competitive edge. Sometimes, when success brings great rewards, the water gets muddied and your original ambition, drive and focus can be diluted. At times like that, your self-belief can be a hindrance. I know because in 2000 I was involved in a plane crash that saw two pilots lose their lives.

By the time I was 30, I had enjoyed a reasonable degree of racing success; I was certainly well paid for my troubles, having raced for McLaren on multi-million-pound contracts for several years. Being completely honest, I was a bit spoilt. I could afford mostly anything I wanted.

I'd just won at Silverstone ten days earlier so I was feeling pretty good. I'd booked a charter flight on the Tuesday afternoon but decided at the last minute that I wanted to go in the morning instead. My usual company did not have a plane available at late notice so they hired another aircraft from another firm. Being impatient to go in the morning was actually only going to get me to my destination just two hours quicker but I wanted to go then – however, we never made it because the plane crashed, killing both pilots.

I won't go into all the details of the crash again because it is obviously very unpleasant and I detailed the full episode in my autobiography. Suffice to say, I had been impatient to get somewhere, arrangements had been altered because of that, and two people were dead. Myself, my girlfriend of the time and a pal suffered relatively minor injuries but the whole incident was obviously horrendous.

That was a life-changing experience and certainly a pivotal period in my life. The plane crash made me question whether I wanted to continue my career path and the answer was 'yes'. It made me realise, far more than at any time in a racing car, the fragility of my own mortality. Because sitting so close to two people who had been killed is about as stark a reminder of that as it is possible to get. I learnt that I wanted to keep racing and I learnt that I wasn't scared of flying because I flew on the Thursday and the crash was on the Tuesday. I wasn't even that scared at all on the next flight. I trusted in the airline and, besides, I had to fly to get to the next race in Barcelona. McLaren and Ron were extremely accommodating and asked me if I felt okay to race; I had a couple of cracked ribs but was otherwise physically okay, so I said yes. Ron very kindly organised a private jet to fly me to the next race from the South of France to the Circuit de Barcelona-Catalunya. With the help of ice packs and painkilling injections, I qualified fourth and ultimately managed to finish second behind Mika. Some people doubted whether I should have raced but for me it was very straightforward: I was fit and I was ready. As I have said many times before, it is what it is.

For me, the plane crash represented a moment of growing up. Successful people and those with money often get exactly what they want. Sometimes this is because they can afford to buy what they want; other times it is because people around them assume they will always win, and so give in anyway. The problem is that this creates a very selfish atmosphere around that person. At the time of my plane crash, I was at the risk of being very much someone who thinks 'me, me, me'. I risked becoming self-centred. That terrible crash was a massive kick up the backside.

In business, I hope you never have an incident as bad as the plane crash I was involved in, but maybe take from that the lesson that you should avoid becoming selfish and self-centred at all costs, not just because it's bad for business, but because it's a sour personality trait to develop. If the day isn't going as you planned, don't fire off at anyone who crosses your path; sit down and figure out what you need to do to make it work. If your plane is late, so be it, hopefully you've done what I said earlier and booked the second-to-last flight and you'll still arrive on time. You must not get lost in your own success; stay grounded at all times, otherwise you just become a selfish, self-centred and negative individual who people will not want to be around, or work with.

This brings me on to the topic of fate. I didn't feel as if I was going to have another plane crash three days after the first one. Obviously, I definitely would not like my final chapter in life to be in an aircraft crash. However, I do believe that if your time is up then it is what it is. That's not to say that I don't think you should try to determine your own path, that would contradict my previous talk of working hard to achieve success. If you believe in fate and think you have a certain amount of time on this earth, then it follows that you've only got so many heartbeats; it follows that an average person's heart will beat a certain amount during the course of a day and that person will need a certain amount of sleep, and you need, to eat and drink and so on. When you analyse how many of those heartbeats are when you are awake and working on achieving your dream, then it really focuses the mind. When my time is up, I'd just like to think that I've made the most of mine.

● ● ●

So how is this relevant to you, assuming you are not an ex-F1 driver and presuming that your career is probably very different from the one which I enjoyed for so long? Well, in my opinion, the points in this chapter are just as universal as the ones we have studied from

Formula 1. Even if your career feels established and successful, you can always look for new opportunities; diversifying is always an interesting option if your job or career is at such a stage where that could be a choice; maybe you have had an unexpected change of circumstances and now find yourself looking outside of the world you have populated thus far. If so, then I can tell you there are some amazing opportunities waiting and there is a very good chance that your skills will be highly transferable. Above all, regardless of what you do now or in the future, you always need to enjoy what you do. You only pass this way once so make sure it is an enjoyable journey.

Talking of journeys, in terms of business I feel like mine is only just beginning. When one door closes... that's when I get busy. So right now, as I write this book, I'm running quite close to full-on capacity with all sorts of exciting projects going on, so I'm not looking to start anything new. However, for certain I know that some of my business opportunities will eventually start to drop away, that's inevitable. Some of the brand contracts will fade away – for example, the Channel 4 contract for Formula 1 ends in 2018. So Whisper will, through no fault of its own, no longer be working on that high-profile production.

However, instead of thinking, *This is terrible news*, I look at that and think of all the time it will free up for me to find a new venture or opportunity. I don't know what that opportunity is right now, but it will present itself at some point. As the change in circumstances gets ever nearer, it sharpens my mind and makes me focus on creating new business. 'How do I support my family? How do I make sure that we've got money coming in? How do I make sure that there is opportunity there?' These are pretty simple questions that you should always be asking yourself.

If you read what I have said in this book, then you won't be surprised to hear that I am always looking for the next opportunity. I am fascinated by the social media and digital world, I see enormous potential there; even though it has already transformed the way we live and work, there is a feeling that this is only just starting. So I'd be interested to pursue something in that area.

Another area that is perhaps more obvious for me, given my background, is assisting younger drivers. I've not yet developed driver management opportunities because of the time commitment I believe it would need, knowing as I do what a driver's life, what an elite a sportsperson's life, entails. I actually have some doubt about the amount of work it would take in terms of physical hours that I would have to commit to do it properly. So, if there's doubt, do nowt, as the old saying goes. But time will tell, when one door closes, it frees up time and that is when I really get my elbows out, so watch this space…

Hopefully you'll have found the ideas and analogies in this book interesting, even if you aren't a big F1 fan. I know my ideas won't be everyone's cup of tea but that's okay, they are just opinions and approaches I have formed along my journey in motorsport and beyond. I hope that these insights into the pinnacle of motorsport will spur you on to take a look at your business or career in a new light, knowing what you now do about the complexity of a sport which I have devoted my life to. Ultimately, I hope that these lessons from my career in F1 will also give you an unfair advantage!

APPENDIX 1
CASE STUDY: THE EVOLUTION OF SAFETY IN MODERN FORMULA 1

One case study that I feel exhibits so many of the ideas and traits that have been discussed in this book is the superb way that Formula 1 reacted to one of its darkest hours. It is unfortunate that, human nature being what it is, we often don't do anything until or unless we have suffered a personal experience; at the San Marino Grand Prix in 1994 everyone involved in Formula 1 had a personal experience when Ayrton Senna and Roland Ratzenberger were killed, and the one thing we all knew was that we never wanted to go through that again.

So what did we do?

The answer is that all the key stakeholders including the FIA, the sports' governing body, the Formula 1 company run by Bernie Ecclestone, and the Grand Prix Drivers Association – effectively a huge team – got together and started to work out how to drive these fatalities down to zero. We all set out to make sure that such a thing never happened again. That was their ambition, their lofty aim, their target, if you will.

You might say, 'Well, that's impossible, because Formula 1 can never be completely safe', and of course you are right. It is impossible to eliminate all risk; but what is possible is to understand why incidents, accidents and fatalities happen, and then to work backwards to make sure that things are done in a different way so that incidents don't turn into accidents, and that even when an accident does occur, it won't lead to a fatality.

As previously mentioned, leadership plays a vital role in this change in culture, and there is no doubt that the leadership in Formula 1 responded superbly by setting out to eliminate fatalities. They spearheaded a complete and comprehensive overhaul of our approach that had to come from the leadership down, otherwise no one else in the team would have bought into it. They did this through having a clear goal, striving to operate at their own highest level, being decisive, maximising teamwork, attention to detail, efficiency and staying focused to deliver a coherent solution. Max Mosley, the President of the FIA, agreed with Bernie Ecclestone that we would change the technical regulations to make the cars fundamentally safer, and also examine the tracks to eliminate the danger points. Within weeks of the Senna accident, the FIA had drawn up a list of the 23 most dangerous corners in Formula 1 and set about having them redesigned or slowed down in order to eliminate the risk of high-speed, high-energy impacts. And since Bernie Ecclestone awarded the contracts to each Formula 1 venue, he agreed that the template for all race tracks should insist on the highest possible standards of track safety, crash response and trauma care if the worst were to happen.

The second step was to empower people to take personal responsibility. Two of the key people who were empowered by Formula 1's leadership to address the issue of safety were Professor Sid Watkins, a neurosurgeon who was Formula 1's chief medical officer, and Charlie Whiting, who is the race director and quite literally responsible for how a Formula 1 race is run. Prof. Watkins had been the official Formula 1 doctor since 1978, and he had the sad job of attending to a number of fatal accidents including Senna's – especially difficult for him because Ayrton was his friend. Bernie Ecclestone now asked Prof. Watkins to review everything concerned with safety, and to work with the FIA to do whatever was necessary to ensure that we didn't have any further fatal accidents.

Charlie Whiting was also tasked with reviewing how we operated the races, including how we could better use the safety car to slow the races down whenever there was an incident, or debris on the track, or even heavy rain, which causes poor visibility and aquaplaning.

Something that Prof. Watkins and Charlie had in common was that either of them could stop a race. They could individually stop a Formula 1 race from taking place at all, or stop it during the event if they felt that safety was being compromised. They were given the absolute authority to do whatever was necessary to maintain safety, even if that meant stopping the show from going on. That was highly progressive thinking. Early on in his job Prof. Watkins did actually stop Formula 1 events because the Air Ambulance was not on station or the correct medical personnel on site. He had a template of what had to be in place before a Formula 1 event could start, and if that was not kept to, he could simply contact Charlie Whiting and ask for the event not to go ahead.

Stopping anything in business is hard to do, and certainly in Formula 1 it's hard to consider stopping a race whenever you have over 100 million people watching live on television. But you have to consider the flipside of continuing when safety has been compromised; the potential outcome is not going to be worth it.

The work Prof. Watkins, Charlie Whiting and their colleagues have done has helped to change the safety record in Formula 1 in ways that we could never have imagined. But none of it would have worked if that attitude had not been applied down through all of the teams, all the Formula 1 personnel, and even our contractors who are on site at the races – people like the tyre technicians, engine technicians and so on – in other words, every role imaginable from the top to the bottom was empowered and engaged. We had to educate people as to why the changes were being made, make sure they agreed to the new way of working, and be certain that it really did apply to every single person. This infused the entire sport with personal responsibility.

Did the F1 'team' create a coherent and workable solution? Well, until the sad loss of Jules Bianchi in 2015, Formula 1 had not seen a fatality since the weekend that Senna and Ratzenberger died. Therefore, up until that tragic point, the people involved in trying to make F1 safe had absolutely achieved their goal of zero fatalities for 20 years – for such a massive sport on a geographically enormous scale, that is an incredible accolade, a very impressive achievement. This evolving period of F1 history provides an ideal case in point to show how all the different lessons and approaches I have talked about in this book – which I learnt myself from the very same sport – came together to produce such a coherent and powerful success for the pinnacle of motorsport. The FIA and all its stakeholders together, as 'Team F1', had actually made a Formula 1 car the safest place to be in the event of an accident.

APPENDIX 2
GUY HORNER
FOUNDING PARTNER OF VELOCITY
EXPERIENCE WITH DC

David used to race a couple of levels above my brother Christian way back when we were all kids but to be honest the most time I spent with him socially was when he was chief usher at my brother's wedding. We spent some time together that day and clearly hit it off. He liked what we were doing at TBA Group, our work ethic and clear sense of fun but also our ambition, and that is when DC said he felt that there was an opportunity in Formula 1, that we could deliver something for brands that other agencies weren't doing, creating brand experiences and live events on a scale that the other traditional sponsorship agencies just couldn't do. So, that's how the idea for Velocity came about.

We've always been a busy business and with my brother heavily involved in Formula 1, I never really chased after or targeted Formula 1 work. However, David approaching me with the opportunity appealed to me: first of all, he's been very successful and is a very likable guy; if you are going to be in business with someone you've got to be able to get on with them, trust them and like them. Secondly, the relationships he has with brands and his standing in the business community as well as the racing community is significant, so there is a lot of respect there. Consequently I have a lot of time and respect for DC, so actually it was a very easy conversation to agree to work together on Velocity. Neither of us really needed to do it, but we wanted to.

In terms of a post-racing career, David is the most successful former racing driver of his generation. He is still a Red Bull ambassador, he has various businesses including Whisper and Velocity, and he is a brand ambassador for a lot of high-profile companies, so his approach clearly appeals to a lot of people.

In my opinion, there are many reasons why DC enjoys so much success in the business world. He is very connected in terms of relationships and in turn he understands what brands need to do and how he can help them achieve that. He is very demanding, as he was with his car, but he does that in an extremely positive, collaborative way that creates an environment where people feel engaged. The way he treats everyone is very noticeable – when he comes into the office at TBA/Velocity he makes the effort to engage with the receptionist, all the people he doesn't work with directly, he goes around the whole business to make everybody feel valued and important. He walks the floor and spends time with everyone, which is something that I think most CEOs could learn from. You could argue he doesn't need to do that, but that's not how he sees it, and it's certainly not how he behaves. In return he gets loyalty, support and enthusiasm, but he doesn't walk round the office chatting with staff to manipulate or manoeuvre people, he is doing it because he genuinely enjoys engaging with other people.

Unleashing people's full capability seems to be something he constantly manages to do. He understands that other people have different abilities and he looks to work with that, he is always looking to other people for their expertise. He is what I would call 'a bigger picture guy'; throughout his racing career he obviously always had engineers or people looking at the minutiae, the nuts and the bolts and the little detail, and he is very good at understanding what they can do with their skills and knowledge and he knows when to dip in and out and when to deliver his own expertise.

He is very ambitious; clearly, with his successful F1 career behind him, he could have taken life a little slower, but he is not like that, he is always looking for the next project. When that appears he is very, very committed. He thinks nothing of jumping on a plane to make a meeting if that is what is required. He wants to succeed in anything he does, whether that's on the race track or winning a contract, succeeding with a pitch, being the best agency, or on a personal level striving to be the best he can be. He is definitely very driven, rather than just waiting for other people to do all the work for him.

Everything he does is underpinned by his lack of ego. For example, like everyone, he is not always right but he is very honest and always open to admit he is wrong or that another method is better. He is a very understated and modest man. I don't think he realises how high-profile he is, I genuinely don't. Whenever we go out for meetings or a photo shoot or anywhere in public, we get stopped in the street all the time. He can be constantly stopping but he doesn't mind, he just has a great way with people. He is a very warm person. He's a glass half-full person. I think that down-to-earth nature comes from his family upbringing and the values his parents instilled in him. He is just a normal guy, with a very extraordinary career. He is as skinny as a rake but eats like a horse, he'll have a pint of beer and celebrate a win. Being a normal guy, he gets on with people on a normal level, not on a Monaco superstar level.

In my opinion, Velocity works well because our expertise is in creating amazing brand experiences and delivering them. David recognises that and his expertise is in terms of the relationships and the knowledge he's got of motorsport, Formula 1 and the relationships with all the brands and businesses he works with, so it is a very complementary relationship. Hopefully, with award-winning events such as F1 Live London, people will agree that the results speak for themselves.

APPENDIX 3
SUNIL PATEL
CO-FOUNDER OF WHISPER FILMS

Starting up Whisper was a huge risk for me personally. I was in a well-paid and safe job at the BBC, I was starting my family and buying a house, there was a lot to suggest it was a mad idea to risk all of that to set up a production company. However, my view was that it is not every day you have the chance to set up a company with a sports star, a businessman who has had success in many areas, and create something new and market-leading. Plus, there was just that kind of glint in DC's eye that meant you knew that this would work somehow. We discussed the idea with Jake and all agreed that if we went about this the right way, there was no reason why it shouldn't work. That said, having DC attached to the project really gave me a level of reassurance that this was the right thing to go and do. It just felt like it was an opportunity that doesn't come around every day.

Our first contract was Williams and, also, we were working with Red Bull right at the very start and we haven't looked back. Obviously winning the F1 contract for Channel 4 was a massive coup but we have also been very successful working with the likes of Channel 5, Olympic Channel, Alfa Romeo Sauber, The FA, Citrix, Formula E, The Race of Champions, Ferrari, Mercedes and Hyundai, among others.

TV is a very different place from Formula 1. If you talk to people within F1, they mostly have the same ethos and culture; that is the way Formula 1 works, but TV is a very different place. It's not as commercially focused, it's not as populated with so many incredibly driven people. TV people are creative people, so that can come with a lot of baggage, a lot of sensitivities and a lot of sensitive souls. So when you come into TV with the driven, ultra-professional approach that Formula 1 uses – an approach that is accepted and certainly works – then there is scope for a culture clash. When you try to apply that with TV it's very difficult, and trying to get people to buy into that approach with Whisper was very, very tricky from an early stage but we have now managed that. We've taken on the best bits of what DC has brought to the company, taken the worst bits of TV out and built a hybrid of the two. The best bits being the constant striving for marginal gains, the focus, the drive, the professionalism of presentation and sense of team, but for TV you have to apply that without being quite so, I guess, brutal. It's a case of marrying the two worlds to create the best of both.

At times there are moments when the hard-nosed F1 world clashes with the softer TV world and DC is very good at filtering that out, at protecting the staff from that level of ambition. He plays that game very, very well and makes you feel part of this journey. He has got a wonderful knack of being able to pull a room together and really inspire the whole team.

David is very driven, very focused, very ambitious. He has the kind of desire that says, 'anything's possible', I know that sounds a bit cheesy but it is true. He gets the right people in place and treats them in the right way, which engenders a collective vision to get the job done. Yet he always comes from a place that is pretty self-deprecating. He is a very successful Formula 1 driver, a successful businessman, but he does like to poke fun at himself. Also, he is always the first to say, 'Look, you guys are the specialists here…' and allow others to do their jobs. But then behind the scenes he is always kind of 'on it', he's always there. He is always on the phone to me, constantly coming up with ideas on 'How can we be better, how can we tackle challenges, how we can work together to make this business work?'

David brings a real professionalism to every element we do. One specific element of Whisper that DC has introduced to a TV production company, in my opinion as an industry first, is the immaculate presentation. So, yes, we run Whisper as a fun and very creative TV production company, but we present immaculately. I would suggest that if you go to any other production company in the UK and walk into the offices, it will be a complete mess, there will be tapes, props and crap everywhere. This often infects the branding, too, so for example different staff send out documents in different fonts and it's all a mess. Whereas what we've done is just kind of pull all that back and work on that image, the presentation, the detail. We now have team kit when we go out and film and that's not really a thing that's been done within TV before. I admit that when we first introduced the idea, not everyone was in agreement, there was an element of 'Why are we doing this? I want to be cool and wear my own stuff', but over time that attitude has changed and people have bought into the vision.

What traits has DC got that business people could learn from? Cutting to the chase, ambition, drive, desire, never laughing off an idea. He will always listen and not dismiss a suggestion, no matter how crazy it may seem. He generates confidence in people and the staff around him. When we said we were going to come out of nowhere and win the F1 contract, some rivals actually did laugh, but DC just said, 'Right, why not? How are we going to achieve that? What do we need to do?' Again, without wanting to sound cheesy, DC creates that feeling within a company that with the right people in place and the right mind-set, backed up with massive amounts of hard work, then 'anything is possible'.

ACKNOWLEDGEMENTS

It is traditional at this point to thank pretty much everyone under the sun, and, I must confess, being somewhat of a traditionalist I really feel I should fall in line. That said, I am also a realist, and, despite being on a world tour for the last 23 years, I have only come across a fraction of this planet's people. That could suggest that I believe in life forms on other planets, which I will get to in my next book!

So keeping my thanks to those I have encountered, I would like to start with expressing my gratitude to all the men and women whose skills and work effort allowed me to follow my racing goals and travel from karting in Scotland through to racing in the world's fastest form of closed circuit racing, Formula 1.

What I have learned along the way is covered in this book, and to bring this journey to print has only been possible by the collaboration of Martin Roach, who was my ghostwriter on my 2008 autobiography *It Is What It Is*, and Mark Gallagher, who I have known since my earliest days in cars and he has continued to be a sounding board of common sense when it comes to the business of racing and Formula 1 in particular. Both men are independently successful in their own right but, like me, value the power of teamwork and collaboration. Mark and I have spoken all over the world, covering subjects ranging from high-performance team work to leadership, data driven performance to innovation, and, of course, driving.

I would also like to thank my literary agent, Dave Daniels from CSA, and my publisher Blink, my editor Matt Phillips, as well as Madiya Altaf, Emily Rough, Karen Browning, Jamie Taylor, September Withers, Justine Taylor and Richard Collins.

My parents, of course, deserve recognition, not only for creating me, but for being so hard-working and committed to achieving their goals together. That commitment to family, business and my karting career laid the foundations of all my future success.

My wife Karen never fails to show incredible patience as I continue my growth through life and she represents more than 50 per cent in our team effort. I love you, darling.

And finally, to the next generation, our son Dayton, who at nine years old has told me he wants to be a Formula 1 driver! Well, son, read this book, and if you have the work ethic, commitment and understanding of how to get the best out of your team, then I don't doubt you will achieve your goal.

INDEX

(the initials DC refer to David Coulthard)